How We Got There From Here

For Roger Street
with best wishes
Virginia [signature]
December '98

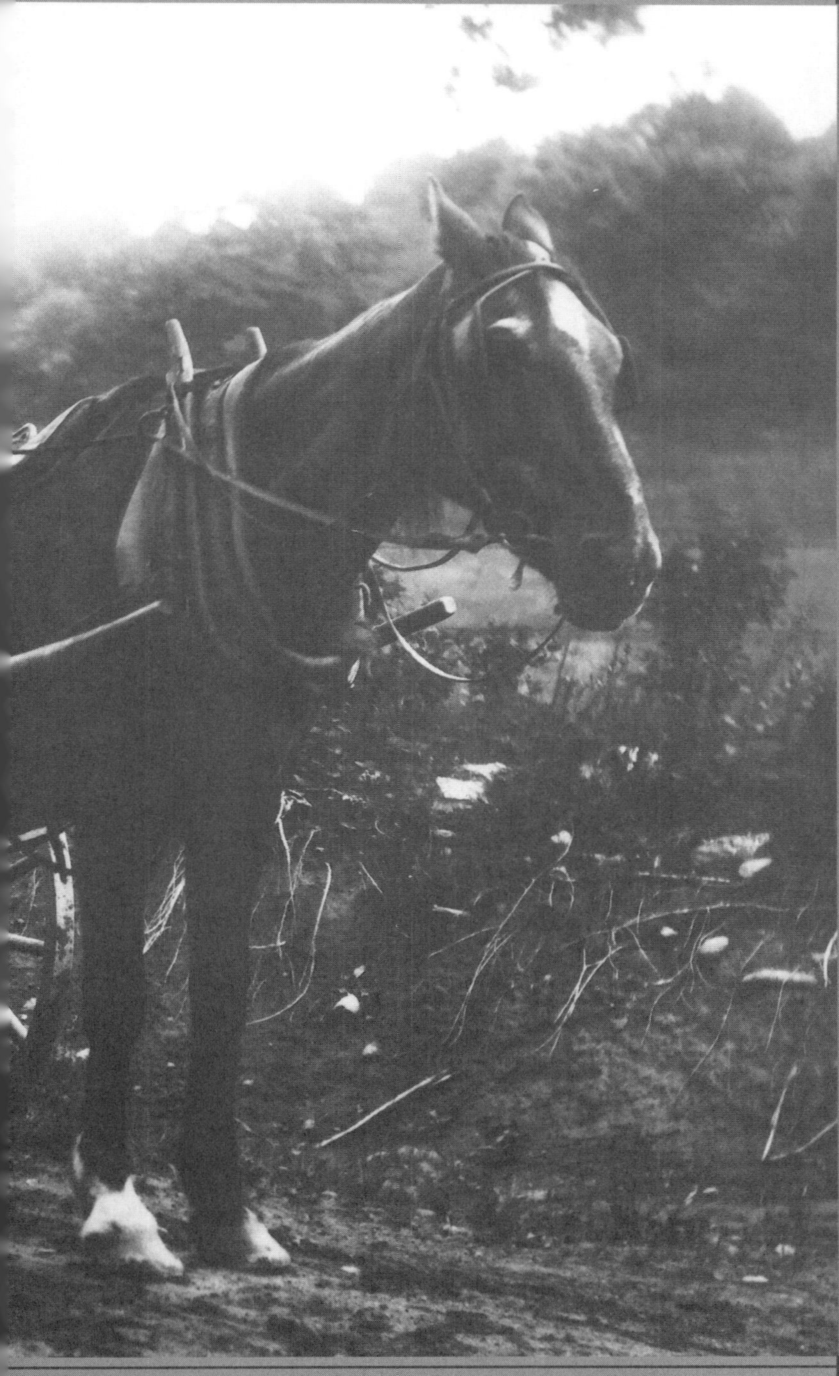

How We Got There From Here

Remembering the Days of Steamers, Trolleys & Model Ts in Maine

PHOTO COURTESY OF LINCOLN COUNTY HISTORICAL ASSOCIATION.

Copyright © 1997 by Virginia L. Thorndike
ISBN 0-89272-410-2

Book design by Lurelle Cheverie
Printed and bound at Capital City Press, Montpelier, Vt.

1 3 5 4 2

Down East Books
P.O. Box 679 · Camden · Maine
Book Orders: 1-800-685-7962

Library of Congress Cataloging-in-Publication Data

How we got there from here

    p. cm.

  ISBN 0-89272-410-2 (pbk.)

  1. Transportation—Maine—History. 2. Transportation—Maine—Anecdotes.

HE213.M2H69   1998

388 '.09741—dc21   98-34922

                                             CIP

To Pebble

This all started with you, who thought I might
put together some old photographs of transportation
in the state of Maine; you gave me three wonderful
ferry pictures to whet my appetite. It worked.
Then I got to thinking about some of the older folks
we'd spoken with during the course of writing
the *Bowdoin* and lobsterboat books, and it seemed
to me that the photographs would be made more lively
with stories told by real people. So here's the book,
even if it's not what you had in mind. Thanks anyway!

Contents

Author's Note viii

Ground-Sparrow Legs 1

How Grandfather Got to Seguin 2

Coasting Schooners 3

Big Schooners 10

Piloting 17

Ferries 20

Everything Was Boats 23

The Boston Boats 27

Small Steamers 32

The Last Sidewheeler 42

Lake Steamers and Other Boats 46

Remembering Stonington 50

Snow *57*

Raymond Oxton and Old Harry *62*

Horses *66*

Working on the Narrow Gauge *82*

Trains *89*

Trolleys *100*

Bessie Dean & Midnight Express *105*

The Transition to Automobiles *108*

Cecil Pierce Reminisces *113*

Automobiles Everywhere *115*

Ray Vigue's North Woods *124*

The Storytellers *131*

Author's Note

Virginia L. Thorndike

"Until I started thinking about it, I never realized how complicated transportation was, nor how simple it was." So said Roy Monroe, of Milo, during his eighty-fourth year.

Nowadays, when we go anywhere short of the moon, we almost always take an automobile or perhaps a plane. Since the taming of the horse, the most significant changes in how people get from place to place have happened within the life span of the storytellers here. There are people in Maine today who can remember when there were no automobiles in their towns. The world is a completely different place than it was when they were born.

I make no pretense whatever to any academic ambition within these covers; this is a series of memories, in words and pictures. In fact, some of these memories may be inaccurate. I decided it wasn't appropriate for me to change what was told to me even on the occasion or two when I suspected something had been misremembered. Nor will I claim that the specific memories recorded are typical of their time—but they're indicative, at least.

Sometimes the subject went afield from issues of transportation, but the people themselves are as much a part of the book as the ostensible theme—transportation—and I have left some of the meanderings in place.

Each of my informants had something to say, and I feel honored to have had the opportunity to listen. I hope they enjoyed reviewing parts of their early lives, but I cannot imagine that they got as much pleasure from it as I did. I am very lucky to have this peculiar wish to collect things into books, giving me the excuse to meet such wonderful people. Thank you all, every one.

It has been a true joy to traipse around finding the pictures, which have come from a myriad of sources, public and private: The Maine Historic Photograph collection at Fogler Library, University of Maine, the Maine Historic

Preservation Commission, Maine State Archives, Maine Department of Transportation, Cole Land Transportation Museum, Bill Abbott, Edward Coffin, Bessie Dean, Doris Hall, Robert MacDonald, Jim Rockefeller. As for the local historical societies across the state, and their curators, you are just the best. You have such resources, you are so willing to share them, and you're so enthusiastic—thank you to Belfast, Boothbay Region, Brooksville, Islesboro, Lincoln County, Lincolnville, Southport, Thomaston, Union, and Yarmouth. I'm sure that any number of soci-

This early ferry was pulled by hand along a fixed cable.
FRANK CLAES COLLECTION.

eties I didn't happen to ask would have been equally welcoming. The service you're providing is invaluable.

I am particularly appreciative of the Southport Historical Society for letting me transcribe their tape of Cecil Pierce, who had passed on by the time I began this project.

As I look back,
that's all a part of my existence,
and it doesn't seem to be what so
many people refer to as olden times.

Isabel Ames
NORTHPORT

Ground-Sparrow Legs

Nettie Douglas
DEER ISLE · 1910s

How'd we get anywhere? We walked—or ran. I never stopped. I went as fast as I could go—never thought to walk. We lived on top of a hill, and I'd run down, help my grandmother do her chores, then run back and do the things to home. I had long legs—I could run. Uncle Harl used to call me Ground-Sparrow Legs. My old feet and legs are gone out on me now, but they used to serve me well. I was hopin' I could see a little better so I could crochet some, but I can't read nor write nor crochet nor nothin', so I just roll back and forth in this chair.

One time we had an awful blizzard snowstorm. My brother Roy loved the snow. On the way home from school, he laid down in the middle of the road and let the snow cover him all up. I said, "Roy, you're gonna get run over," but he'd just get up and shake himself and lie down again. He didn't have to worry about horses—nobody had horses.

We had to carry all our water. There wasn't water in the house. Oh my, no—never thought of such a thing. There was springs all over the island, but in a real dry summer we had to dig in the cedar swamp and scoop the water out in cups and fill a bucket and carry it home.

My brother Robert was born club-footed and couldn't walk till he was three years old. Where would you take anyone like that for treatment back then? So my father brought up pieces of kindling from when they was buildin' the vessels and tied them on Robert, straightened out his feet, and put plaster of Paris on the top. Now they have those tongue pressers. They'd be some nice to use for splints.

Did I ever go anyplace as a kid? Well, I went to Stonington once. My father was down on the vessel, and he said I could come along and stay with my aunt in Stonington a week or so. She had two girls there, Ethel and Florence. I stayed a night, but then I thought, by gorry, I'm not going to stay here. I stayed with my father on the vessel for the rest of the week. I hadn't ever been to Stonington before, but I'd have found my way home again if I'd had to.

How Grandfather Got to Seguin

Cecil Pierce

SOUTHPORT ISLAND · 1910s

About the time the two silly brothers down in North Carolina was tryin' to prove to the world that man could fly like a bird, I was born up here in a tar-bottom dory. These are not my words exactly—"he was born in a tar-bottom dory" was a common phrase for a person who was knowledgeable about the water, born to be knowledgeable. (They say it about a Nova Scotiaman a little differently—they say he was conceived in a dory, standing up.) So when I come ashore from the dory—'course I could row a boat then and swim—I landed in this town of Southport, and I want to tell you how crude this town was in those days. There was no doctor here, no telephone, no electricity. Automobiles hadn't proved themselves yet, and we had no roads that they could travel on anyway.

It'd be a decade ahead before we had any of those things, two decades before we had electricity. So perhaps in the early days I could best tell you how crude it was by this example.

My maternal grandfather, Albert Orne, worked for the United States Lighthouse Service as a repairman for anything wood—the homes or the slipways for the boats. He traveled from station to station within his bounds. I don't know how big his bounds was, but I don't think he went west of Seguin. But I'll tell you how he got to Seguin. The island is about nine miles from here as the crow flies. So he got a letter in the mail from Roy Luther in Portland saying that some people from Philadelphia were going to the residence out to Seguin, so he ought to go out and fix it up.

Grandfather had a big toolbox, took two men to carry it, so he always took a helper with him for that reason and for the reason that he needed a helper anyway. The toolbox was kept at Cozy Harbor. He couldn't phone Payson to tell him to get the toolbox, he had to walk down to Payson's a half a mile and engage him to come with his horse and pick up the toolbox. So Payson would come and take the toolbox over to the steamboat landing, and he and his helper and his toolbox boarded the boat for Wiscasset. Then they set the toolbox in the train to get to Bath from Wiscasset. Or perhaps they went directly to Bath.

Somehow they got to Georgetown; I don't know how, probably by mail carrier with horse and wagon. Well, when he got to Georgetown, he hired a dory, and he and his helper, usually his son, but sometimes another man in town, they'd row on to Seguin, no matter what the weather, almost, and that's a hard place to go, so they tell me. He'd keep the dory there till he got the job done, and then he'd reverse the procedure to get home.

We think today how easy it'd be to go anywhere. Just pick up the telephone and someone'll pick you up.

Cecil Pierce.
COURTESY OF EVELYN BLAKE.

Coasting Schooners

Robert Billings
DEER ISLE · 1920S

The *Mercantile* was launched when I was nine years old. They built her mostly in the winter months. They had to work summers to get money enough to buy the equipment. Pearl (my father) and his brothers Arthur and Walter built her. Dad was with the previous vessel he'd built, the *Enterprise*, for income during the summer. They built five altogether. It took them three years to build the *Mercantile*, or it could have been four. In the summertimes she set there and cured. Wintertimes they put her together. I never worked on it, I weren't old enough. Oh, I helped maybe with the shavings bag and like that. But I did work on the last one, the *Billings Brothers*. They built the *Billings Brothers* smaller, with hopes of putting power in her, but she was sold when she was quite young. Never had a motor in any of them. They'd have to had a license to operate it if it had power, and none of them did.

They used yawl boats. On *Mercantile* they had a five-horse, single-hitter motor, a Mianus. Gasoline.

We'd be out six weeks or two months, something like that. Like to go to Gloucester, you could make it in a couple of days, but you had to go according to the weather. We went from Swans Island to Gloucester, Massachusetts, carrying fish. We returned with salt. The *Mercantile* carried a little under one hundred ton of salt. We carried other things—a load of brick from Orland, coal and pulpwood and hardwood and lumber—a lot of different things.

Robert Billings.
COURTESY OF THE BILLINGS FAMILY.

Schooner Mercantile *loaded with pulpwood, headed for Bangor, at Old Maid's Creek, Gouldsboro.*
COURTESY OF ROBERT BILLINGS AND MAINE WINDJAMMER CRUISES.

The C. M. Gray *taking on a cargo of wood.*
COURTESY OF
CAPTAIN BILL ABBOTT.

She drew about seven or seven and a half feet loaded, but only about three and a half light.

We had to read the weather the best we could. We had to have it smooth so that the wind would be offshore and we could make our trip. We went once with the wind heavy nor'west the second day, then she changed and went to the east and out into the southeast, instead of going southwest. Before we reached Kittery, a great big bank of fog was comin' in on us. We was close enough to the harbor that we could see the buoy, but we had to guess at the speed we were making where we turn there and enter the harbor. We never got caught in the fog to be lost altogether, though. We were always in sight of shore. Well, from Kittery to Cape Ann you couldn't see the land, but you knew where you were in the bay.

We were caught in a snowstorm one time, when the *Mercantile* was turned over to my older brother, Sidney, and myself—Dad was incapacitated some way. We went from Rockland to Boothbay in a nice chance of weather. We went out of Boothbay. I talked him out of it the first day—it was northeast—but we were anxious to go, and we went out the next day. We got way out past the Cuckolds, by Small Point—beyond return—and I said "Give her the best sheet you can, and take a look at Halfway Rock, and put it on your compass so you can see, and we'll guess at our speed." The farther we went, the harder it blew, and there was no way to know what speed we were goin'; it was all guesswork. We could go—we had to go, we couldn't have gotten back if we'd have tried. So we give her the best sailin' we could.

Before we got into Portland we had about two inches of snow on deck, but it weren't thick enough but what we could see our traveling. We made Halfway Rock and the entrance to the harbor, and we went in.

We had a compass and a barometer and a set of charts, that's all—we knew where we were all the time. We very seldom sailed at night. Sidney did, that last trip I was tellin' about. The first day it blowed hard, and they stayed right there in Stonington. The second day they went out and got off Portland. It was nice enough to go, and they discussed it between them: "We were in and wished we was out, and now we're out and we're wishin' we was in. Let's see if we can let her go." (What we were scared of is a southeaster storm. A nor'wester wouldn't bother us because we'd run under the land, see.) They got her goin' and went right into Gloucester, so they were out there all night.

This trip that Sid went with us, she was loaded with salt and was layin' off Billings Beach when she dragged ashore. She dragged the big anchor with sixty fathom of chain and grounded out. 'Course they had the whole chain out, but it weren't in the mud, it was down on the rock, and the peak on the anchor broke off. Dad had to watch her all night. The next morning when we went down you couldn't see a hundred feet in the vapor over the marsh, but they knew where she was. They went out and saw they had a split rudder. So they had to jack that back around again and put a plank on the side of it to keep her straight. At high tide she went off. They went right into Swans Island that night.

They took three or four days to hoist the salt out of her. There was no power. They'd push it into big tubs and hand it to the guy on the dock, and he took care of it from there. Aboard, we took care of it ourselves.

It took another five days to load fish, and then they went into Stonington. Well, the next day was a heavy nor'wester so they had to stay there, but when they went out, they made it right through, one day and one night and half of the next day, straight course.

The fish would load way up high under the deck, and if it took six weeks to get there, it'd be way lower. All of that settling, we'd pump it out. That was the pickle. It was so quick from Swans Island that Dad called Ferd Morse, where we took the fish from, and said, "I'm in Gloucester. And, oh, boy, am I some pleased. We sold them twenty ton of salt pickle water," because it hadn't drained out.

One time we were way down Old Maid Creek, close to Gouldsboro. You went way up in the creek to a little bit of a dock. You could lay there in the mud and load her, but you couldn't get out until the high tide. The creek was like a snake's back, you know. At night you couldn't tell where the channel was, so the afternoon before, we got alders, gitchel birches, anything with little twigs on the top that would make a pole ten or twelve feet long, and we made perches in the daytime and set them out, here, over here, over there, over there. When the captain ordered, I'd take a pocketful of matches and a bunch of newspapers and light a perch and mark it. The yawl boat was runnin' the *Mercantile*. I was rowin'. When he gave orders that he could see it, I'd row as hard as I could for the next one. We had about three miles of it to get out to deep water.

We knew enough to keep on going to the anchorage. I rowed aboard and tied up and had a night's sleep. But we went from there to Bangor with pulp to the paper mill. Then when we were tied at the dock in Bangor, the Eastern steamship was comin', and we had to hurry onto the *Mercantile* to watch the ropes. When the steamship come in to dock, it turned around and made such a surge that it could part the lines.

My younger brother, Lloyd, and I were sailin' one time. I was in charge. Dad was home. I was probably twenty-one or twenty-two, and Lloyd was two years younger. Al Shepard was on the *Enterprise*. Dad left orders, "If Shepard goes out, you chase him," Dad bein' responsible for both. If anything happened, I'd be right with him.

I went in to Portland and Al stayed out. I went up to the dock and tied up, and then he come in and tied alongside. See, the thing of it is, the tide goes up and down, but he don't have to bother his lines. I had to have the lines to keep both of us.

Then we started out at daylight. We were towed out by a towboat. The days are short in December. But I outsailed him, and I had to go back and back and come back, until we'd gotten three-quarters of the way, and I could see the other end, then I could let her go and be in the harbor ahead of him. We were towed by a towboat right into Gloucester.

We had a four-cupboard Shipmate stove, burned wood and pea coal. We burned pea coal in the winter, night and day.

We were in Swans Island all loaded with fish once, and Ferd said, "You wouldn't be interested in a car, would you?" Dad, Lloyd, and I bought the 1917 Dort from Ferd, and Lloyd took it to drive it, and they went out for about an hour. When he brought her back, we got some plank and at high tide we put her on the *Mercantile* in the middle of the deck between the foremast and the mainmast.

We took her sailing to Stonington, and put her in to the dock, and put the plank down, and Lloyd drove her right up.

Captain Bill Abbott
VERONA · 1930S

I can remember the *Stephen Taber* hauling pulpwood. A lot of schooners were taking pulpwood then—that's all they were being used for, those days. Well, the *Lydia Webster* used to haul bricks from Gross's Brickyard in Orland. I can remember seeing her, because her masts raked. They had quite a rake to them.

My father piloted small tankers up and down the river. One time he was on the *Irene Allen* or the *Justine Allen*, and they were coming down at night, after they built the bridge. All those lights on the bridge would shine down and blind you. There was a schooner chugging along up the river—I think it was the *Mercantile*, but I'm not sure. He had his sails up and had his boat pushing. His wife was in bed, and he was steering. They didn't see the schooner. They just got through the bridge, and they run into her, or she run into them. Anyway, her foremast went down, and they towed her into Bucksport. I don't remember an investigation by the Coast Guard, but the fellow sued the owners of the *Justine Allen* and the *Irene Allen*. He said his wife hurt her back falling down, and he claimed that he had the right-of-way, because he was sailing, but they decided where he'd had his yawl boat running, he was under power, and there was no fault found.

Parker Hall used to keep his schooners across from where we lived, in Gunlow Cove. It's called Gondola Cove on the chart, but Gunlow Cove was the local name for it. He had two schooners, and he'd stay aboard of them. He used to keep them there in the winter—ropes and things running ashore to the trees—and the ice would build up around them, and they'd freeze in there. One time there was a big rainstorm. I'm surmising it was a southeast storm, because that would make a high tide and break up the ice, and it would blow them out of the cove. Anyway, they broke loose and drifted out of the cove and down to

Schooner Stephen Taber *in the 1920s. Sometimes the vessel would be loaded with as much as sixty-three cords of pulpwood.*
COURTESY OF CAPTAIN BILL ABBOTT.

Mattie, one of the first dude schooners, with a deckload of passengers. Before being switched to the passenger trade in 1938, she hauled cargo for more than fifty years.
COURTESY OF CAPTAIN BILL ABBOTT.

Fort Point Cove. Captain Harold Spurling and the tug *Walter Ross* went down to get him, and they towed him up to Bucksport and tied the vessels up for the rest of the winter.

He was an awful bowlegged fellow. Wore big hip boots and that made him look even worse. He stuttered awful. I remember up at the store in Verona, some guy had Parker in tow and was making a telephone call for him. Parker was trying to tell him what to say—bananas, it was. Funny, the things that come into your mind.

We were going to help him raise sail one time, and we grabbed onto the halyard and our feet just come right off the deck. "B-b-b-boys," he said, "that's n-n-n-not the w-w-w-way you d-d-d-do it. P-p-p-put your h-h-h-hands up over your h-h-h-head and your a-a-a-ass right straight down."

Gertrude Frasier
VERONA

After I had finished my nurse's training, I sailed on one of the dude schooners two summers. By then, Captain Hall was captain of the *Mattie*. He stammered, you know. Every story he told, if there was a villain, it was a damn Dutchman—a d-d-d-damn D-D-D-Dutchman. The cabin boy was named Dickie, and Captain Hall'd stutter a lot when he said Dickie's name—except when he

wanted the boy to do something in a hurry. Then it came right out. He always had to come in to Sandy Point on Thursday nights, I think it was. They had dances there, and he had to get to those dances. He was ninety then. They had a mate on board with a full license, because there was no way to know when something might happen to Captain Hall. That was in 1941 and 1942. In 1942, they couldn't go outside like they could before, because of the war. They had to stay inside the islands.

Moving Day

Robert Billings

My aunt Rhoda moved from Deer Isle down to Stonington in 1918 or 1919, I think it was. They moved all her things in the *Enterprise*—they had a yoke of oxen, so they put it up in crates and carted it down and loaded her up. They put her out into Swain's Cove. They called me up or notified me somehow, and I went aboard and stayed all night. Rhoda's husband, Shep, got up about four in the morning or earlier. He milked, and we yoked the oxen up and put them into a hayrack, with hay and bicycles and whatever else we could carry. The rest of it he had on the *Enterprise*.

Percy, my cousin, and I took the oxen down. We had to yoke them up and get them all ready, and as soon as Shep was done milkin', we tied the cow behind and hurried to go all the way out to the marshes way down beyond Deer Isle and onto the bar, because we had to go across on the low tide. We had about eight inches of water to wade through. If it had been any later, we wouldn't have gotten across. We fed the oxen as soon as we got across the bar, because we didn't take the time before or we would have missed the tide. Then we walked down to Stonington. All the roads were gravel and dirt then. The next day, one of the oxen got up in the morning, but the other one didn't get up till afternoon, he was so tired.

Daniel McCobb's Move to Boothbay

Excerpt from a poem written by P. Helmrich of Alna, April 30, 1916.

DANIEL AND HIS ARK

Daniel's ark has left our shore;
It was heavily loaded from aft to fore.
The household goods were packed in snug,
With the old family teapot wrapped in a rug.

The cattle yokes of which we knew,
Were counted exactly twenty-two.
The ark was loaded with lumber galore.
We believe Daniel will build on the other shore.

The goose and gander were packed in a crate,
Voicing their remonstrance at a two-forty rate.
The pig with her squeal and crook in her tail
With a grunt was placed at the forward rail.

The cattle in turn took their place near the mast,
While a crate of hens and a rooster came last.
A load of hay was stacked near the cattle's abode
And the hungry critters ate up the whole load.

Big Schooners

Harold Bunker
1920s

Rena and Harold Bunker.

PHOTO BY VIRGINIA L. THORNDIKE.

OPPOSITE PAGE
An unusual view of the four-masted schooner D. H. Rivers, *taken from the end of the spanker boom.*

COURTESY OF JOHN ELLIOT, WHOSE GRANDFATHER TOOK THE PHOTOGRAPH.

When the Eastern Coast Company was fishing out of Rockland, I made twenty-three to twenty-four trips till they folded up. We were in those trawlers tied up at the dock, and a fella came down, a captain, wanted eleven or twelve crewmen to go on a five-master out of Bath, the *Gardiner G. Deering*. She'd been tied up there a long time. I was only a kid—fourteen, if that. I went out as cook on her for twenty-one men. All hands were green except the captain and the mate. I borrowed a cookbook from a woman who ran a restaurant in Rockland. I didn't know nothin' about cookin'. I wasn't nothin' but a kid. I could run a coal stove, though. I'd run a coal stove since I was a child. You can't let it burn up too far before you shut it down, else it all goes to ashes.

We had to get that vessel all ready, but before we left, the boys took the alcohol out of all the compasses. The captain got awful mad and went tearing around on deck, but he didn't dare fire us because it was hard to get a crew.

That night come on a northeast snowstorm and a gale of wind, and it started to ice up. Below deck, there was a lot of water—we run both pumps on her. He run her dead reckoning and come into kind of a lee and let both anchors go. I thought the bow'd come right offen her when they went. We had to cut the sails offen her.

We laid in there a couple of days, getting more sail on her, and then headed off toward Boston. Another gale of wind come up, and a pilot boat—a schooner—come and towed us off Massachusetts somewhere and let us go. We anchored there in the lee, and the captain went ashore on the pilot boat. We were out of tobacco, and we told him to get us some—we was smokin' newspapers, everything.

The next day a tug come out of Boston and towed us in. We were leaking bad—the damn thing was about half full of water. We had two of them big steam pumps going all the time. And we didn't get no tobacco.

They said they'd caulk her, but they only caulked her from the water up. We laid there three or four days and started eatin' up the food pretty fast. The captain come down and was lookin' around, askin' where this was and where that had gone. I said I'd been feedin' the crew.

"You ain't s'posed to feed all that to the crew. That's for the aftercabin." That's the captain and the mate, you know.

"I thought we was all just alike," I said, but he didn't want to take me any further. The boys said they wouldn't go unless I went cook, so they all decided to leave. We packed our bags and walked. They went their way and I went mine. I

10

The Gardiner G. Deering, *built 1903.*

FRANK CLAES COLLECTION.

didn't know where the hell I was going. We didn't get no money. We'd signed articles for Bath to Norfolk, Virginia, where we were going to take on a load of coal and then head back to Bangor. We weren't going to get no money until we'd made the whole trip. But they all decided to leave except the second mate.

I got a job in a factory making Lux flakes, runnin' this big machine. I had a lever and had to keep the temperature just right or it'd harden up. A lot of guys, you'd have to go out in the yard and chase them down, but I stayed on my machine.

After a few months, I was itching to get back to Matinicus. I told the boss that I was leaving at the end of the week. Mr. Carlisle his name was, in charge of twenty-eight hundred people. He wanted to know what I was leaving for, and I told him I wanted to go lobsterin' again. He said that if I stayed on, they'd send me to night school; it wouldn't cost me nothin', and I could work days. But I decided to leave, and I went home. I had money, I'd been working long enough, so I took the steamer back to Rockland, the *Camden*.

When the *Deering* come back from Norfolk to Bangor with the coal, that same trip, they unloaded her and she died right there.

Arthur Hall
1920s

I used to go along the coast with Captain William Merritt, my stepmother's uncle. There were a lot of places along the coast that had little two-masted schooners. They worked just like trucks, today, taking goods along the coast. Uncle Will—Captain Merritt—was from Addison, Washington County, and he started out as a twelve year old on one of those little schooners.

He told me about the ice trade. Four-to six-masted schooners would load up at the big icehouses on the Kennebec River, and they'd go to South America, to those packing places. Captain Merritt told me they'd take all those big schooners and use hawsers and tie them fore and aft. Then with two big steam tugboats, they'd take them down the river. All the crews were taking bets about who would get out of the bay first. One after another, all the schooners would drop off and make sail and see who could get out first.

Uncle Will went to sea for the Deering company in Bath for many years; he sailed the *Carroll A. Deering*, a five-master. He used to go on a regular run from Portland to Newport News, Virginia, carrying coal for the Portland Edison people. One of those big schooners could carry a tremendous amount of freight.

One time as he was leaving Portland, he had an appendicitis attack. His next-oldest son was mate, and going along just for the trip was Captain Thurlow and his son. Uncle Will was going into the hospital, so the owners said it would be okay if the Thurlows took the *Deering* to Newport News, just this trip.

The *Deering* never got to Newport News. She was sighted by a lighthouse on the trip down with only one of her anchors; she was missing one. She later turned up on the Diamond Shoals, all sails set, food on the table. She'd just drifted in—she had no power. It was one of those mysteries like the *Marie Celeste*—she was found sailing around, crew gone, food on the table on her, too,

Tug Bismarck *with a tow on the Penobscot River.*
COURTESY OF CAPTAIN BILL ABBOTT.

BIG SCHOONERS 13

not a thing wrong with her. They never found out what happened to her or to the *Deering* either, though the papers said bootleggers got her.

Uncle Will figured it out, though. Those big schooners carried a yawl boat on davits, and he thought what they did was go over the stern on the yawl boat, and as they came around the stem, she hit them and rolled them over.

During World War I, he was carrying coal in the *Dorothy Bennett*, a four-masted coal schooner. There were German subs all around the coast. One surfaced on the leeward side of her and shot across the bow and told them to abandon ship. Uncle Will'd had German mates in the old days, all good sailors and good guys, and he thought he'd tell them he had no war supplies and they'd let him go. The submarine submerged and came up again on the windward side and took the foremast right out of her. So Uncle Will and the crew took the yawl boat and left her.

As he was coming in, a Coast Guard patrol boat stopped him and asked him to take them back to where the *Bennett* had sunk. "They're gone by now," Uncle Will said. But the Coast Guard said, "No, let's go." So they went. The Coast Guard was pretty new at this. There was an explosion—they thought they were being shot at. The skipper walked back and forth on the bridge with his revolver out. But it was their own deck gun, firing at their own wake. Uncle Will said it was a pretty frightening experience.

There was a lot of traffic on the coast in those days. When I was fourteen, Captain Merritt had a great big schooner they'd bought on the West Coast and brought around through the canal and up. He was loading coal in Boston and was going to take her to South America. He said I could come along with him, and I was very excited. The mate was a Finn and he had a big scar, from knife-fighting probably. Uncle Will left me in his charge and told him, "Get that yard down. It'll be getting in everyone's eyes, not setting sail." There was a single yard on the foremast with a single course, zip up the middle of it—you could haul out half of it, if you wanted to. It was West Coast sort of stuff. They'd go out to Hawaii and places where you could use a rig like that.

She had a steam donkey engine, and the mate put me in charge of that, which was rash. The mate knew his business, though, and I was pretty fascinated with what was going on.

But the trip never happened—the owners failed.

It's probably just as well.

Parker Marean
WISCASSET · 1933

The *Luther Little* was white and all rigged up. Chippy Chase and I, early in June, looked it all over. There was a guy on board taking registrations. They were supposed to take a case of stuff down from the narrow-gauge railroad and bring coal back for the train. But there was a wreck on the tracks June 16, 1933, and that was about the end of the railroad, so they didn't go.

The Wiscasset Schooners

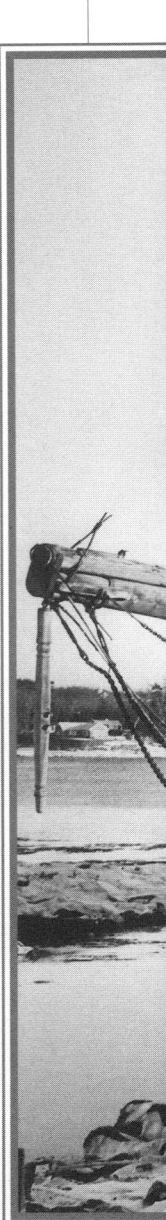

14　　　　　　　　　　　　　　　　　　　　　HOW WE GOT THERE FROM HERE

Karl Edstrom and the Hesper

(Notes by Gordon Bok: A few years ago the friends of the Wiscasset schooners were trying to raise funds to "stabilize" them. They received a letter from Karl, who had sailed on *Hesper* when they were both young. Someone went to the nursing home to tape his recollections of those days. It was from this story that Lois Lyman made the song and put it to the tune "The Swarthfell Rocks.")

My name is Karl Edstrom, I am eighty years old,
And I heard that you're trying to save the *Hesper*.
I joined her crew in 'twenty one—for Le Havre we were bound—
I was twenty then, and I will never forget her.

She was cloud-white and long, and her four masts so lofty
That her topsails seemed to pierce the sky above her.

The Hesper *and the* Luther Little *in 1968. Generations of travelers across the Sheepscot River bridge watched the two hulks slowly collapse into the mud.*
BOUTELIER PHOTOS.

BIG SCHOONERS

She was strong and deep and wide, timberports on either side;
When I looked at her, I thought that she was lovely.

We sailed out of Rockland with a crew of nine men
And her hold was just as full as we could pack her.
She was loaded down and slow with logwood and coal
And her bottom was so foul we could not tack her.

Caleb Haskell was master and the mate was his son
And a tougher bastard never sailed blue water.
For no matter what we tried he would not be satisfied,
And he drove us all the time we were aboard her.

When we landed in France the dockside was swarming
With pedlars and ladies so charming.
"Where are the men?" the ladies cried; they could not believe their eyes
That only nine of us had brought her to this landing.

The cook got so drunk that we all ate on shore
And I thought the Old Man would hire another,
But the captain said, "Let him be, for he's sober out to sea,
And he makes a better pie than my mother."

Rolling out to Venezuela we sang and made music,
Played cribbage, killed rats and stood our watches.
We arrived on Christmas day, over New Year's we lay,
Loading goat manure until it reached the hatches.

In Charleston, Carolina, they paid off my time.
I said good-bye to my mates and there I left her.
It's been fifty years for me since I made a life at sea;
Now and then I think of Haskell and the *Hesper*.

So here's my ten dollars to help you restore her
For it makes me sad that ships like her are gone now.
But it grieves me even more to see her rotting on the shore
Who rode the waves like a snowy gull in summer.

(©1988 by Lois Lyman)

Piloting

Captain Bill Abbott
PENOBSCOT RIVER

My father was a ship's pilot. When vessels come into the bays and harbors, they have men that go aboard and guide the ships in. It's a real old profession that dates right back to biblical days, so all along the East and West Coasts there's pilots that bring the ships into the harbors, rivers, ports. My father was a pilot, and piloting was a part of my growing up. I've been on the river quite a while myself. I started piloting in 1946.

My father had a rowboat, a dory, and I remember rowing out with him and getting aboard the tanker. They heisted the boat right aboard. On the Socony boats, they had a little wheelhouse amidships. They had a three-tone whistle, and they could play a little tune with the three notes, so they called them the piano boats. I remember the *Bacoi* better than any because that was the first ship I ever stayed on all night . I don't know why we anchored. We went up just above Winterport and anchored and then went up the next morning, and I slept on the boat with my father. The galley was way up forward, and I can remember being there for breakfast. It was all smoky, with bacon and eggs and a checkered tablecloth, and boy, it smelled awfully good and tasted awfully good.

We went up to Brewer, to Eastern Corporation. In the wheelhouse when you got ready to dock, they locked in another steering wheel, and to do the docking we went up on what they call a flying bridge, another bridge higher than the regular wheelhouse so you can see all around and see what's going on.

In 1910 the Maine Central Railroad opened a big coal-digger tower in Bangor to supply the Maine Central and the Canadian Pacific with coal. They

Tug Walter Ross *with a light four-master on the Penobscot River.*

COURTESY OF CAPTAIN BILL ABBOTT.

brought in two hundred and fifty thousand tons a year. The tower paid for itself in one year. Each boat carried five thousand tons and took sixteen hours to discharge. They had a bucket that held one and a fifth tons in one grab, and it grabbed every three minutes. The facility operated until 1933.

The coal was brought up by steamship from Newport News or Norfolk. They had a number of lakers—you know what a laker is? The pilothouse is forward. She'd have a pilot aboard, Captain Bennett or my father. They'd get on at Fort Point. They'd take a draft of probably twenty-five feet to Bangor. The dock at High Head—that's where the Veterans Bridge goes across now—had a depth of water of twenty feet at low water, the deepest berth in Bangor. They'd start up the river two or two and a half hours before high water. They had to get over the famous sawdust bank just above Bucksport. It took a couple of hours up. They'd get up at slack water, and they had the tug *Walter Ross* to help them dock if they needed it, or to help turn around. They'd go up one day, and they had to dig out before low water so she wouldn't ground out, and they'd come back out the next day.

A lake steamer carrying coal by Odom Ledge on the Penobscot River, ca. 1923.

COURTESY OF CAPTAIN BILL ABBOTT.

They used to bring pulpwood from New Brunswick in little steamers, to the Eastern Manufacturing Company and Seaboard Paper Mill. The mill got a towboat and made the old schooner *Helvetia* into a barge—used her to tow pulpwood. *Seaward*, the tug was—used to be a passenger ship. We used to call her the *Seaweed*, just in fun.

The *Bismarck* was built in 1888. Old Man Ross had her built special for towing on the Penobscot River. He wanted a boat that would tow like hell. She was wood, steam-screw, carried a crew of seven. She was fast, too—probably about twelve knots. She had an eagle, painted gold, two feet tall. She worked here until about 1910. She went to the Kennebec for awhile, and then to New York, and she was scrapped in 1926. She was the Queen of the Penobscot River, under Captain Bill Bennett. He blew to everyone along the river. He was a great one for salutin' people, much to the chagrin of the firemen—you had to keep up a head of steam for that. They could crow like a rooster with the whistle. My father was mate on her. He done decking, firing—everything—and worked up to mate. Bill Bennett left towboating in 1910. Lumber and ice schooners were slacking off, and he could see the end comin'. He went to piloting and took my father with him.

• • •

Roy Meade was a pilot here who did a lot of docking of ships in Searsport with Captain Harold Spurling on the *Walter Ross*. My father did the river work more. Roy Meade was a big man, and when he got along in years, his leg was all bent up with arthritis. They got him up on the bridge with a ladder, and he'd sit on a stool and dock the ship. Coal boats ran steady into Searsport at the C. H. Sprague dock for the Great Northern Paper Company.

There was one ship ran there a lot, and they were gettin' ready to undock one time. It was a windy southwester in the afternoon. Rather than get Roy up on the ship and get him back off on a breezy afternoon, the captain said he'd do the undocking, and Roy'd stay aboard the tug. They pushed and backed the ship out and then moved up on the bow to shove the bow around, and the captain let the towboat go. He was all finished with it. Roy dropped back, but the ship was swinging onto him, he couldn't get out of the way. The captain had hard left rudder, and she scraped right down the side of the towboat. The ship was light—floating high in the water—and her prop cut a hole in the side of the towboat. They went full ahead and beached her against the Sprague dock. Just as she fetched up, the water was up even on the webbing in the engine room floor. Sprague took good care of them and welded patches on to keep her going till they could get her into drydock. There was no great damage done, and nobody got hurt.

If Roy had been on the bridge, would that have happened? You can't tell. A pilot can make a towboat look awful good or awful bad. That's one of the tricks of piloting, to get the most out of the towboats. They could do some bad things. They could get in irons: The bitts were well aft, and when they towed a barge and it sheered off to the side and took control—that's getting in irons. They've rolled towboats that way. The newer ones can't do that, the bitts are closer to amidships.

Captain Don Rogers
1940s

Comin' home from New York I stopped in Portland and was settin' on the dock looking over at the pilot boats. A fellow saw me there and he ended up offering me a job. You know the windjammers down to Camden? I was engineer on the *Timberwind*, down there when she was a pilot boat. Her name was *Portland Pilot* then. It was a good job. I liked it, though it was rough. She had those two big diesels aboard her. She'd go up one sea—go up that way, forty-five degrees. Then she'd go over the top and down so fast it'd make you sick to your stomach. But that's the way it was out there. I fell off the mast in 1942. I still got a bump on my leg. It's a wonder it didn't kill me.

There was one time—I wasn't aboard her—they had a pilot with a stiff leg, and he was climbing up onto a freighter. It was rough, and he called down, "My God, I can't make it!" and he fell, and that was the last of him.

I got twenty dollars a week all found. Bought a car—paid twenty-three dollars for it. It was good money, those days.

Ferries

Gertrude Fraser
BUCKSPORT · 1920s

When we first came from Massachusetts in the car, the roads weren't all paved, and usually we'd get three or four flats and stop and take the tire off and patch it. The high bridge over to Verona wasn't there then; you had to take the ferry to Bucksport. The other side of the fort, the road went steep down to the ferry, and the ferry was nothing but a scow. It had sides, but nothing on the bow or stern because you drove on and off. It was always after dark when we got here, and if we were the first ones on I always used to worry. I was afraid we'd fall in the water.

Captain Bill Abbott

They ran ferries across the Penobscot River, Bucksport to Prospect, until they built the bridge in 1930. The scows had motorboats on them to push them. They'd push them over, turn them round, and push them back. They didn't have any clutches. When they'd come into the dock, they'd pull the switch and watch the flywheel, and when it came up just right, they'd pull the switch again, and then she'd back down.

Ferry leaving Bucksport for Prospect, before 1930.
FRANK CLAES COLLECTION.

Margaret Libby
1920s

The ferry from Verona to Bucksport was open as early as possible in the spring and as late as possible in the fall. If you really had to get to Bucksport in the winter, there was a bell you could ring and someone over on the other side who had a motorboat would come over and pick you up. Sometimes it was scary—the ice cakes coming down at you, and with the current you'd sometimes find yourself going down the river instead of across it.

Roy Monroe
1920s

The *Bon Ton*, that was a river tug up in Bangor and Brewer. You had to step down considerably to get on it, and after a while, it would take you to Brewer. If you were fortunate, it would come and take you back; otherwise you waited for the railroad. There was no bridge open to traffic at that time.

Went Durkee
ISLESBORO

There wa'n't no cars on the island till 1933. They fought it a long time, the summer people did. Theirs were the first to come on, once they allowed it. The first ferry was Lee McCorison's old scow, the *Redwing*. He'd come in on the mud

Murry Clay on the ferry between Bucksport and Prospect, 1925.

FRANK CLAES COLLECTION.

at low water, stick two or three planks down, and you'd drive down on the beach, everybody pushin' to beat hell to get you on. He used to land you right on the beach in front of the garage in Lincolnville, and I can tell you, it took some pushin' to get up the beach. There might be someone there with a horse to pull you up. That old scow had two Dodge car engines in her. Took two or four cars, I don't remember for sure.

I'll never forget when they brought the first scheduled ferry here, the *Governor Brann*. It was the clumsiest thing you ever seen. Built like a chopping tray. They could bring her into the pen, and she'd turn around right there. She was just about round. The sea'd come right in on deck two feet deep, and it'd all just run right off again. Can you imagine the purser walking around with hip boots, collecting fares?

Mel Trim, first selectmen, said, "We'll never see the day she won't carry all the traffic here." In three months, they took her to Rockland, chopped the middle out of her, and stretched her out to make her take more cars. And they've been fighting ever since to keep ahead of it.

Everything Was Boats

SOUTHPORT ISLAND

Everything was boats, in those days. We had a neighbor over here who rowed to Bath once a week for his groceries. He'd time it so he had a fair tide going up and a fair tide coming back—goodness gracious, it's twelve miles. It was an all-day proposition. It'd be stupid to come back with the tide against you—you might as well sit in your dory and wait for the tide to turn, you'd get back the same time.

The steamer *Winter Harbor* used to bring the mail from Wiscasset to Boothbay Harbor. They made two round-trips a day. There could be nothing more monotonous than that. I've been on her when a fellow from Westport rowed out and met her and put in an order, and then when the *Winter Harbor* got back again, he'd get his order off her. He was smarter than the guy who rowed to Bath.

It used to take a long time to get up here, by steamer or by train, and then we used to come up by car. That took twelve hours in those days. I always enjoyed it. I don't think we improved anything when we went to trucks. What do we do with all that time we save?

I always wanted to be a native, and my mother knew I wanted to be a native. It's a mistake on her part that I'm not, and one she's not easily lived down.

My father taught at Boston Latin School, and we came up here summers. He had decided we should have our own cow, so when I arrived, at the age of three months, so did the cow. The poor little cow was bought in Dedham, Massachusetts, and it took them all day with a horse and cart to get her down to Eastern steamship wharf in Boston. She was nervous and bellering, and I was hollering. I wanted to get to Maine, and she wanted to go back to Dedham.

Eliot Winslow

Captain Eliot Winslow.
PHOTO BY VIRGINIA L. THORNDIKE.

Steamship Wiwurna.
COURTESY OF THE BOOTHBAY REGION HISTORICAL SOCIETY.

23

Then we had that long ride down on the *City of Rockland*. We got to Bath in the morning, and they transferred us to the *Wiwurna*. It wasn't much of a job to move us from one ship to another, but the *Wiwurna* had a lot of stops in those days: Upper Westport, Lower Westport, Riggsville—that's now called Robinhood—Macmahan, Five Islands, Isle of Springs, Sawyers, and finally Southport.

Well, that's a long ride, and the cow and I were having a hard time. And worst of all, it was a low, dreenout tide. And you know when it's a dreenout, full moon or new moon: there's all that gangrene stuff showing, and it's awful slippery. The cow took one look at that ramp down there on the Southport wharf, and she wasn't going to move. She braced herself with all four feet. Someone suggested twisting her tail, and they tied it in a square knot. But that didn't do any good; it just got her all nerved up. The captain said, "I'll blow the whistle, that'll do it." So they blew three blasts on the steam whistle, and that upset the cow. She threw up from both ends to once, and what was slippery was worse than ever. She got her tail in it and slatted around. They had to close the windows in the pilothouse. Then they decided to put a rope around her horns and get all hands to yank her out. So they took a half hitch on her starboard horn and went down under her tail and come up around the port horn and took a hitch around that. Everybody in town was there at the landing. They knew my father was bringing home a new brat and a new cow, and you might say he knew nothing about either one of them. They hitched the lines and everyone started dragging. Well, she resisted just as hard as she could, and she clobbered herself, oh, dear, how she clobbered herself. Those four spigots that every cow has were all mashed to pieces. The result was she gave gargety milk all summer long—gargety milk is milk with copious amounts of blood in it. My father always said that was my trouble ever since.

When I was seven or eight years old, I used to row up across the bay to Love's Cove, to a farmer named Graves. I'd tie up to a tree, walk up to his house and get the milk, and row back. It was a lot shorter by boat than by foot.

But my rowing career ended abruptly. I had a girlfriend on Boston Island—she came summers. I used to row out to get her, row to Robinson's Wharf to the dance hall, row her back, and row home in the wee hours of the morning—all for a peck on the cheek. Well, I got her in one night, and the fog came in. I had no compass, no real light. I was in my neighbor's dory, standing up to row. A third of the way home, I found the buoy I wanted, and I figured if I rowed just a little harder on the right oar, I wouldn't go out to sea. Well, I rowed a little too hard on the right oar, and I went right around in a circle. I finally came ashore at five in the morning. I walked along the shore until I got to what I thought was a boathouse, and I stuck my flashlight in the window, hoping to see a lobster buoy and see where I was. Well, there was a man living in there, and he was some upset. My poor mother said, "You ought to know better. All for a silly girl." The girl married a guy with a fast boat and a compass, and that was the end of my romance.

I wasn't old enough to go down and shovel coal on the steamers, but I was intrigued by them. You'd see a guy all sweaty, and you'd think "What a rugged guy he is." You'd want to be like him. The last time I was on a steamer it was in World

Dories are reliable, efficient rowing boats. Here Jim Pitcher uses a dory to bring in a couple of traps.
COURTESY OF THE BOOTHBAY REGION HISTORICAL SOCIETY.

War II, and they'd resurrected four old ore-carriers from World War I. They were laid up when they activated them, and they used them as weather ships off Greenland. There was a fear then that Germany might invade Greenland and hop over and invade Canada. The Germans did land some people on Iceland and Greenland, but they were all rounded up. We had a simple code that most any person in that business could decode. That was our assurance that the Germans wouldn't sink us, because the information would be useful to them, too.

I was navigation officer on the *Menemsha*. She had a vertical stack—that's a sign of old age. She looked old, she made seven or eight knots, and she burned coal and put a smudge all over the horizon. Navy headquarters would tell you to take evasive action, but how can you take evasive action when all you can do is eight knots downwind? It's like telling a one-legged man to run. We had no guns—couldn't run, couldn't fight. There was no chance of escape if you got hit; she'd fold up in the middle and go down like a clam bucket.

There was one ship on duty all the time, one coming, one going, and one in the repair yard. It's like a WPA job. It takes four guys to do a one-man job: one going to the toilet, one coming back, one in the toilet, and one working. One of them did go down with all hands. They didn't even have a chance to get a message out. Her name was the *Manasquam*.

Wasn't that a miserable job, those guys down in there, shoveling coal by hand, wearing nothing but a set of skivvies? But as a kid, it used to intrigue me. At night, when that stoker'd open that fire door, the fire would illuminate his face. You saw the flames reflected in his face. It was quite a sight.

I used to like the smell of the steamers. They burned soft coal, and you could also smell the lube oil. They were always lubricating—the pistons ran up and down, in sight. The engineer ran on bells. The captain rang that bell, and, boy, you had to work fast. If something went wrong, the engineer always blamed the captain for ringing the bells too close together. It's easy to do when you're all excited.

Steamers and a schooner wintering at Robinson's Wharf, Southport Island.

COURTESY OF THE BOOTHBAY REGION HISTORICAL SOCIETY.

Right at Robinson's Wharf, they stored vessels for the winter. It's pretty deep water for a small cove. Five or six steamers wintered there. It's well protected. I keep my tugs in there. The *Bowdoin* used to tie up there, and she outfitted there. Maynard Robinson, who owned the wharf in those days, was not a good public relations man. He couldn't get along affably with the summer people. They'd come along, and he'd say, "Here comes another silly question about the *Bowdoin*," and he'd try to hide behind a barrel or something.

How'd I start in tugboats? I got into the navy and that stuck with me. Everybody in the navy was going to have a hen farm, as far away as they could get from salt water. It worked just the opposite with me. I went and got my captain's license in the merchant marine and went to sea a few years and then got into towboating.

The Boston Boats

1920s, 1930s, and After

Albert Chatfield

In the early years, we'd come up on the steamboat that sailed from Boston at five in the afternoon. The first stop was Rockland, at five in the morning. The boat carried mixed cargo—boxes and barrels—as well as passengers. The Boston to Bangor boat brought produce in and took manufactured goods out. The next stop was Camden, and then it went on to Belfast and Bangor. It would come back down the river and be back in Camden at seven at night. Then it would leave Rockland at nine, from what's the Coast Guard station now. There were two boats running. The last ones were the *Camden* and the *Belfast*.

Steamship Camden *on the Penobscot River, ca. 1925, from Dorothea Dix Park.*

COURTESY OF THE MAINE HISTORICAL PHOTOGRAPH COLLECTION.

Went Durkee

The summer people would call an order into S. S. Pierce, in Boston, and the next morning by six o'clock their stuff'd be on the wharf.

Captain Bill Abbott

They used to run the steamers until cars and trains took over. It was quite an event to go and greet the Boston boat when someone you knew was coming. Some passengers brought their cars aboard. They had a great red carpet they ran out for the passengers to walk on or off the ship. The only passenger ships left when I was a boy were the *Camden* and the *Belfast*. I never had a ride on either one of them. They were triple screw. The center one only went ahead, but the two outside ones backed. I was told they used to have to slow down to make their schedule into Rockland. Or if they got behind, they could most always catch up.

We used to go down on the shore to see their waves. They made quite a big wave. We'd sit in a rowboat and ride over the waves, or if we were swimming, we'd run and jump in the waves.

Captain Don Rogers

I've been on the *Belfast* once—my mother and I went when I was maybe five. We took off from the dock that used to be over here and went down to Camden. On the way down, Captain Alfred Rawley come by and shook my hand. I can remember him just as clear as anything, and he's been dead for years. He lived up in Winterport. He was a great man.

Captain Eliot Winslow

You could set on benches overnight. It was a luxury to have a stateroom. Those wooden vessels would creak and groan. You couldn't sleep if you weren't used to it, because you'd wonder when she was going to fall apart.

Schedule of the Bangor Line, 1915.
FRANK CLAES COLLECTION.

Margaret Libby

I went on the Boston boat one time. We had relatives in Dorchester, Massachusetts, and they invited my mother and me to come down and spend a few days. My aunt lived in Bucksport, and she decided to go along too, with some of my cousins. We took the Boston boat out of Belfast. I was about ten. We took a picnic lunch and left Belfast around three in the afternoon or a little after. The reason I can remember it was such a beautiful afternoon is that we sat up on the top deck and ate our sandwiches. In the stateroom there was a little wash basin in the corner and bunk beds—not really inviting. But the next deck down was where the dining room was, and it was pretty extravagant. There were white tablecloths and brass spittoons everywhere.

We got into Boston the next day. I wasn't very much impressed with Boston. Where we went was a triple-decker apartment building, and we were on the top floor. There was no place to play; it was very confined. They did have a tricycle, and I rode it on the sidewalk. We did go into town for dinner to a restaurant there. It seemed as though it was very noisy. It was all foreign to me. A neighbor asked me how I'd like to live in Boston all the time, and I said, "Oh, no, there's no room."

Coming back, it was stormy and a lot of people were seasick.

Richard Sexton

I used to come up and stay with my aunt in Camden whenever I could. She liked to go fishing and was very much a boy's type. I never rode on the *Belfast* or the *Camden*, but when I was old enough to drive my aunt's car, a great many hundred years ago, I used to meet people at the boat. You didn't have to worry about knowing if it was on time or not, because you could hear it blowing its horn all the way up from Rockland.

In the fog, it was really something. The boat was 320 feet long, and it would come in by what was called Negro Island then—now it's Curtis Island. They'd get about halfway in, and they'd be practically stopped. A little man would go out in a rowing boat with a thing beside him on the seat that he pumped back and forth; it made a squawking noise like a fog horn. When he let go of it, it stopped, fortunately. He would row a little way, stop and pump on that squawker, and then row a little farther in. He guided them right in to the dock from that little boat.

Doris Hall

Did I ever ride on the train? Not when I could go by boat! While I was teaching, I would take courses at Boston University during the summer. I would take the boat at five o'clock in the afternoon, and six dollars would give me a room with two berths in it. I would be in Boston at seven the next morning. The boat ride was wonderful.

One time when I was coming home, there were some young people I knew with me up on the highest level, just under the officers where they were steering the boat. "Look, girls," I said, "over there. It looks like there's a boat on fire!"

Then we heard one of the officers: "Hand me the binoculars! She's right!"

We left our course and went over to the boat. Here were these two people in a rowboat, a man and a woman, getting swamped. "How would you like a ride to Maine?" the officers asked them, but they weren't interested. "All right, we'll send the Coast Guard after you." But that's how it was: everyone would go out of their way for someone in need.

They used to have trouble once in a while. They'd blow the horn in foggy weather and listen for the echo to know where they were. Sometimes there'd be a smart aleck on shore—there's always a smart aleck in every generation—and he'd get a hold of a horn and keep blowing it. First thing they knew, they were headed for the mainland. But they always were able to catch themselves, and there were no disasters.

Gertrude Fraser

Which would I choose, the car or the boat? Oh, the boat, the boat! But it wasn't up to me. The boat was fun. We used to leave Boston at 5:30 in the afternoon. My father worked at the Gillette company then, and he got off work at five. We'd come in on the trolley and the elevated, and I was always sure we'd miss the boat. But we didn't. We had a stateroom always, sometimes two. They had upper and lower berths, and over in the corner was a little metal sink. We usually took a lot of fruit, and I think we got breakfast on board, but I was only about ten—it was seventy years ago—and I'm really not sure. The first stop was Rockland, early in the morning, just at daylight. We used to like to get up and watch them take freight off. All they had was those two-wheeled carts, and there was a steady stream of them coming off.

Arthur Hall

When I was in boarding school in the late twenties, I'd take the Eastern Steamship Company night boat, the *City of Bangor*, from Boston to Bangor. The

Steamship City of Bangor *in Belfast.*
COURTESY OF DORIS HALL.

30   HOW WE GOT THERE FROM HERE

captain used to travel at twenty-one knots, fog or not. We'd come into Rockland, and there would be all the little steamboats bobbing about, waiting to take people out to the islands.

There was one turn where a pine tree hung right out over the river. The captain used to stand on the outer end of the bridge, where he could wave the man on the wheel this way or that, and he'd always drag the ensign through the outer needles of the pine tree.

Roy Monroe

I rode a short distance once on the Boston boat that used to run from Boston up Penobscot Bay. I have strong memories not about the vessel, but about the approach to it. There was a long ramp with long planks laid crossways, and as you went down it, they'd ripple as if there was water under it, which there wasn't. Looking back, you wonder how anyone got out.

Abbott Pattison

A few times, maybe only once or twice, we came up on the boat from Boston, the *Belfast* or the *Camden*. It was a real adventure, to get in a cabin and sleep on a boat when you know you're going through the ocean. I was between nine and fourteen, probably.

"There goes the Boston boat!" you'd hear through the house every day when they went by. To see that ship coming down the bay in late summer, with the lights on—it looked like a big birthday cake. There weren't many big ships in those days, not like today with all the ships going up to Searsport and all.

During World War II, I was captain of a PC subchaser, a 175-foot ship with a crew of seventy-five men. I was called in and told I would be escorting two troop-carrying ships, the *Comet* and the *Arrow*, from Honolulu to Midway Island. It turned out those ships were the old *Belfast* and *Camden*, which had passed by our house every day for all those years. They'd been refitted to carry troops and looked like sardine cans. All the cabins and railings were covered up with steel. There were no apparent windows.

Jim Greenlaw

The *Camden* and the *Belfast* were exactly alike. When I was in the service, I got into Honolulu and saw a boat there, and I said, "I recognize that boat!" Now I don't to this day know which boat it was. It was the only time I ever saw her over there. But I knew it was her, even though they'd changed her all over. There was enough there so I knew.

Smaller Steamers

Albert Chatfield

They had little steamers, too. When the Boston boat got into Rockland from Bangor or Boston, there were a half-dozen little steamers there. The *J. T. Morse* went over to Bar Harbor and stopped several places along the way. They went through the Thorofare and stopped in North Haven and Stonington. One went to Castine, one sailed to Blue Hill, and another went to the westward, I'm not sure how far. Perhaps to Bath.

I remember there was a wedding in the family—my uncle and aunt's son's wedding. They had five children, and this was nearly the youngest. He was married over in Winter Harbor. The whole family went over there by the *Morse*, then we took a smaller boat—practically a ferry—to Winter Harbor and stayed in a summer hotel over there. The whole thing lasted several days.

Steamship Nahanada *at Hell Gate, on the Sasanoa River.*
COURTESY OF THE BOOTHBAY REGION HISTORICAL SOCIETY.

Captain Eliot Winslow
SOUTHPORT · 1920s AND 1930s

At the town landing in the summer, there'd sometimes be five or six steamers coming through: the *Southport*, the *Westport*, the *Catherine*, the *Nahanada*, the *Wiwurna*, and the *Samoset* all ran here. Some people would come down on one and take another steamer to Monhegan. I remember going out to Monhegan on the *Novelty* when I was in high school. It was still a rustic island, unspoiled—America one hundred years before. It was a place to go for the day, just the way it is now. It was famous for its artists in those days, just as it is now. You'd get on at Boothbay and in an hour and three-quarters or two hours you'd be there. It's eighteen miles, and if you asked, the boat'd go into Christmas Cove and pick you up. Well, that added three-quarters of an hour at least. They could make nine or ten knots, but it could be a sloppy trip in a sou'wester.

Going to Bath, they had to have two men on the wheel when they went through Hell's Gate. There was an S-turn, and when the current was running strong one man couldn't turn the wheel fast enough by himself. It was all right when the tide was slack, but when it was running five or six knots, you'd have to turn 180 degrees in the length of the boat—that's why you'd see two wheels right together, six inches apart: one man would take the spokes of one and another man the other. I don't know how they did it, 'specially in the fog, but of course you're so close to shore through there. You're not more than fifty or seventy-five feet from shore all the time. But the government fixed it; they blew a rock out, and you can go straight now.

Raymond Pendleton
1920s

I worked on steamboats for three summers. I was in high school at the time. They ran year-round, and in the summer they took on extra help. I was part of the extra help. I started as an errand boy in the Eastern Steamship office, and then I took care of the baggage room. I was on the *Southport*. She went down through Dark Harbor and up to Castine, one trip a day. They used to take passengers to Castine, summer people mostly, and then coming back they'd pick up a load of sardines and bring them back to Rockland and transfer them to freight cars. They'd take quite a cargo of them. The second year, I worked on deck. We used to truck those sardines aboard and off again with a hand truck. They were large cartons, maybe fifty pounds. There were three of us on deck.

The third summer, I worked on the steel-hulled boat *Pemaquid*, run by the Maine Central Railroad. She was housed in Rockland. They had a railroad track that went all the way to the wharf, and they'd take summer people right down to the boat. That steamer went to Dark Harbor, too, and then through the Reach to Brooklin and Blue Hill. Those summer people had a lot of freight. They brought a lot with them, because for the people going to Dark Harbor, that's the only way they got things over there.

Steamships frozen in at Tilson's Wharf, Rockland, 1905.

FRANK CLAES COLLECTION.

As deckhands, we used to truck the stuff aboard, and I remember there was one job I didn't like. One deckhand stayed ashore every day, and he had to shovel up seven tons of coal from a coal car into bucket cars, like wheelbarrows, that would hold a half ton of coal. Those would go aboard at night, ready for the next day. You could load the shovel as full as you wanted to, or as light—it still took pretty much all day. Kept you busy, so they knew you weren't idle. Everybody took a turn except the mate, of course, and the purser. You got pretty good money, though, for those days.

One time when I was working for the Eastern Steamship Company, a summer person came aboard. She was walking around on deck, and a seagull let go on her hat. It was a very expensive wool-trimmed hat, and she didn't like that very well. And another time, the purser and I got in an argument over something, and the crew made us settle it in a wrestling match. I don't remember how it came out.

We didn't get very rough weather, really, because we were inland, but I've seen it rough enough to come in on the gangways on the side. They'd button those up when it was rough, and I've seen the water come in there. But it was all inland water, so it didn't get that bad.

Fog? Oh, yes. An interesting thing was going through all those islands—you could get off course and get on a rock. Those captains could tell how close they were to the island by blowing the whistle and hearing the resound. You had to be in the pilothouse or in the bow to do that, and you had to be acquainted.

Ralph Colby
1930s

The *Southport* made the Blue Hill run in the summer, from Rockland to Islesboro, down the Reach to Brooklin and up to Blue Hill. In the winter, there weren't so many passengers or so much freight, and they'd lay up the *Morse*, the sidewheeler. This fellow was too big—'specially in ice, which would tear those paddles all to pieces. They'd lay up the *Southport*, too, and put on the *Westport*. She was just about like the *Southport*. I went over to the *Westport*. Not all the fellows did, because she had a much smaller crew, but I went.

On Monday we'd strike out and go to Bar Harbor. We'd lay there overnight and come back Tuesday. Wednesday we'd go on the Blue Hill run, go down and stay overnight and come back. Friday we'd go back to Bar Harbor and return Saturday. Sunday we'd lay over. Not in the summer, though. Then we ran seven days, so we worked seven days. Most people were a little different than they are today. There was only one or two of us not married. Some of them used to take a trip off, sometimes, I guess. I never did.

Jimmy Skinner

In 1940 and 1941 I was cook on steamboats. It was a private company that ran two boats: the *North Haven*, year-around, and the *W. S. White*, strictly a summer boat. The navy bought the *W. S. White* and took it to Port-of-Spain, Trinidad, but I didn't go with it. I could have, but I didn't want to. I'd had enough of it by then.

I couldn't boil water when I got on. My father-in-law got me the job. He worked at a market in Rockland, and I guess he kept seeing the fellow who owned the steamers. He asked if they had any work for me. "What can he do?" Mr. Stinson asked him.

"I don't think he can do anything," my father-in-law said, but they said they'd give me a try. They put me with this old guy—name was Hamblin, I think—and he was a pretty good cook. He'd been a chef in New York.

FOLLOWING SPREAD
Steamship North Haven **docking at Iron Point Wharf, North Haven.**

FRANK CLAES COLLECTION.

HOW WE GOT THERE FROM HERE

SMALLER STEAMERS

Well, this one time he said, "I'm going to let you get breakfast all alone. I don't think you can do it, but we'll just see." He was watching from his bunk, and when he saw all that burnt bacon coming out, he jumped out of bed and threw it all overboard and pretty near threw me with it. But he said, "You need the job, so I'll help you out," and he brought me pies and so on.

I couldn't cook beans worth beans. They were all hard, and they'd throw them at me. Get one the back of the head and you'd feel it. I had a coal stove, and I didn't know nothing about that thing. My mother had cooked everything in the world on a coal stove, but I never paid any attention. It went out one time, and I poured kerosene on it. It blew the covers up through the roof nearly. I learned about that. It was awful hot work in the galley, but they had two guys shoveling coal into the boiler, and that was really a hot job. I was the only one there—you had to do your own dishes. You'd warm the water by steam. You'd turn the handle and it'd go *crack*, *crack*, and *crack*, and it wouldn't take it a second to get it boiling.

Steamship Norumbega.

FRANK CLAES COLLECTION.

I'd come down to the boat about three in the morning and start getting ready. The guys were mostly Vinalhaven guys, and they slept on the boat. They would be asleep when I got there, and when I'd start rattling dishes around, they'd want to beat me up. I'd get breakfast on the table about five, after we left Rockland.

In the *White*, we made two trips a day to Carvers Harbor, on Vinalhaven. There were buoys out there then, just like there are now, and you'd run from one to the next. The fog would be so thick, you'd run into it before you ever saw it. They didn't have radar or any of that then—the captain used to go by listening to the sound. Down through the Thorofare it was very narrow, and they'd toot the horn and listen, and that's how they knew where they were.

There was a lot of baggage going out to the island—everything for the stores out there. There were a lot of sardine factories over there, too, so we brought back barrels of fish. There was quite a lot of business in the old days.

You know how the tide is. Well, a stevedore had a hand truck with a couple of hundred pounds on it. I think they'd hook him to something to haul it up, but going down it was like he was shot out of a cannon—about went overboard on the other side. I never worked the hand trucks. That scared me. They must have been going forty, fifty miles per hour down there!

Lunch we'd have back in Rockland. I'd feed the wharf crew over there. There was one guy took care of all the orders as they came down. I had him for dinner, and the boss came down for dinner, too. He probably preferred the other boat. He was a great cook.

You cooked everything, whatever they had. One guy, all he'd eat was bread and butter—that suited me fine. I cooked pies, biscuits. We must have had stews and so on, but I don't remember it. I did the shopping, and if I went over forty-five dollars, I had to go through a big rigmarole to see what I'd spent the money on. They were hearty eaters—all big people, too. I wished they'd eat a little less. It wasn't a job I enjoyed. I did it two years, and that was long enough. But anything was good after the lime company.

I don't remember an icebox. Funny, too, because I used to be an ice man, when I was in high school. I delivered to all the stores in Rockland, and to houses, too. They had a card they'd shove up in the window to let me know they wanted ice. In the winter I cut ice out on Chickawaukee.

On Sunday, I didn't have anything much because it was the day of rest. Just sandwiches and ice cream. I'd make the ice cream on the way out—crank it, you know. I worked for $17.25 a week, seven days a week. Left my house and walked down to the boat at three in the morning; got home at seven at night.

The *North Haven* did both runs in the winter, going to Vinalhaven, North Haven, and Swans Island. That was mostly passengers—they didn't have so much freight, though they had some. Sometimes we stayed out on the island in the winter. I had a stateroom then. Just a little room, but it was comfortable enough.

I went into the service in 1944. After boot camp, I was happy. They said I was going to be stationed in Portland. 'Course it didn't work out that way, but they took me out on the *North Haven* to a base they had on one of the islands off Portland. It was funny—I told the guys, "I used to work on this boat." Then, before I could let my wife know what was happening, I'd taken off for Africa, and nobody could tell her anything about it. It took the Red Cross two weeks to find out what had happened to me and tell her.

Bill Orr
FALMOUTH · 1920s AND 1930s

There was a store in Portland called Johnson's Public Market, the equivalent of a supermarket today. It was painted orange. We lived in Portland in the wintertime, and we had a summer place out here at Town Landing. At that time, it was all summer people—there were two houses built to be year-round, and the rest were summer cottages. Now there are only about two cottages not converted to year-round. The Casco Bay boat stopped at Town Landing, and the women would get aboard the boat. In those days there was a trolley that ran from Portland out to Freeport, to the Castle, but for some reason the women didn't want to take the trolley. I think maybe it was just a good outing for them, taking the steamer. So they'd get on the boat in the morning and go into Portland, and they'd walk a couple of blocks to Johnson's Public Market, and they'd do their shopping. The store would give them a ride back to the boat. The deckhands would load their groceries aboard, and when they got back to Town Landing, we kids would be there with our little carts to meet them. We always knew how many of them had gone to town, so there might be six of us, or sometimes only two or three. There's a wicked hill that comes up from the dock—it's a death pull all the way—and we would get paid a nickel for delivering their groceries home.

Captain Eliot Winslow
SOUTHPORT · 1926

The *Brandon* ran from Portland to Boothbay Harbor. One time, she smacked right into the fruit store down on the wharf. I remember it well, 'cause I went over to see how far she went into the wharf. The captain gave her half astern, and the engineer thought he gave her half ahead, so she kept right on going—right into the oranges.

Went Durkee
ISLESBORO · 1920s AND 1930s

We came over from Nova Scotia when I was fifteen months old. I don't remember too much about it. It was easy to get here—you got on a steamer in Yarmouth and went to Boston. You'd jump on another boat to Rockland, and then another to Dark Harbor.

We always went on the steamer to Belfast or Camden. There used to be four or five boats a day to Dark Harbor run by Central Maine Railroad and Eastern Steamship Company. And Perry Coombs, who had the *Castine*, used to start in Camden and go to Smith Cove, Bayside, Belfast, Pripet, Ryders, and Castine. Then he'd reverse the whole damn thing and go back to Camden in the afternoon. In the summer there was a mailboat down from Camden at noontime. We had three mail deliveries a day, in those days.

I don't remember how much we used to pay to go ashore from here, but

Steamships M&M and Eldorado at Bath.
COURTESY OF THE BOOTHBAY REGION HISTORICAL SOCIETY.

you could bring back all the freight you wanted. Long as you carried it yourself, they didn't charge you any extra. We didn't go unless we had to. Maybe once a month.

Parker Marean
WISCASSET · 1932

The *Winter Harbor* came up from Boothbay Harbor twice a day. She sank right at the dock. Up till a few years ago, you could see her down there—parts of her, anyway.

The Last Sidewheeler

Ralph Colby

Ralph Colby.
PHOTO BY VIRGINIA L. THORNDIKE.

The *J. T. Morse* was the last sidewheeler around here. She worked good. She wouldn't roll, but she'd pitch. The paddles on both sides would keep her from rolling, but she'd pivot on them and pitch when the sea was coming straight on. A lot of times, even in the summer, we'd come 'round the hills, from Bar Harbor to Seal and get a sea. Then she'd pitch quite a bit. I was only on her a year, then I went on the *Westport* in the winter. When the *Morse* quit in 1932, I shipped out of Boston and New York for ten years.

The steamships were a good way to travel. They ought to bring them back, but I don't s'pose OSHA would allow it. We did work pretty hard on them, but it was just an ordinary day for us. We lived right aboard and got seventy dollars a month—for the times, though, that was right good money. When I got to Boston as an Able Bodied, I only made $57.50—'course you got your board there, too. If you wanted to go home or see your family, you'd just quit and find another job. There was none of this six months' vacation or two months on and two months off, like they have now. Yes, it was Depression time, but I never had a problem finding a job. If you worked, instead of settin' around not doin' anything, you had no problem.

As I say, I had my Able-Bodied ticket, but on the *Morse* you wasn't a sailor—you was a freight handler. There was seven or eight deckhands doing the trucking. We had those two-wheel hand trucks, and we carried a lot of freight. If local freight was on the wharf, we'd truck it aboard, and then take what come off the Boston boat. You had to load it even, and sometimes you were pretty well right full. You had to make sure you didn't have something for North Haven—the first stop—way in the back there.

They had one of those same trucks aboard, only it was a big fellow—fifteen hundred pounds on it—and it would balance the ship. The passengers would all run over to one side to look at something, and the paddlewheel on that side would be down there digging. The other one wouldn't be digging so much, and it'd raise hell with the steering. So you had to roll that truck way out in the wings. Once a week or so—we'd rotate around—you had to work that job. You got to know what the passengers was goin' to look at, so you'd be all ready. It'd be all fine goin' across the open water 'cause there's nothin' much to look at, but then for instance you'd come up to Stoneton and they'd all have to look at the lighthouse on Mark Island. Stonington, I guess it is, but we called it Stoneton.

The paddlewheels were hitched on a straight shaft; they didn't work independently. It was a big shaft that went right across the whole boat down on the freight deck. It didn't turn very fast—we used to get right on top of it and walk, and it was a comfortable walking speed. You could hear them paddles pounding, thumping. If she was heeled over, the one under water was thumping and the other just a-splashing.

We used to go up and steer once in awhile, too. Goin' from Rockland to

Bar Harbor I don't think there was a course they steered over twenty minutes, and some was just a minute. Steering the *Morse* wasn't much different than any other ship. She had a steam steering gear that pulled the chain. But in a breeze, with those paddles, she was a little more cranky. All they had for equipment was a watch in their hand. They threw a course at you, in points, down to eighths or quarters. You'd hang onto that maybe a half a minute, then they'd haul you over to another one. It's a wonder they did as good as they did. A lot of trips they was runnin' in fog, some of it pretty thick, and they really didn't get into too much trouble. The old sardine-carriers was the same way, and they went into all kinds of gunkholes they'd never been in before. Today there's all kinds of equipment—depth-finders and radar and GPS—and it seems they're in trouble all the time.

Comin' out of Stoneton, goin' through York Narrows, was tricky, 'cause the *Morse* was quite wide, and she almost took up the whole channel. In 1930, there was a schooner at anchor in there, and before they come to, the bowsprit come through and cleaned off the staterooms in back of the house. But she was built in 1905, and she only run into trouble just two or three times. One of the Maine Central boats run into her down by Stoneton off Mark Island, and there were a couple of other times.

But when I was on her, 'bout the only trouble we had was all those spar buoys—they was big, but they'd lay right down on the water at times. They started changing them for cans and nuns like they use today. A couple of times she'd get in a tide and drift down. Them buoys was just wide enough to catch in the beckets. It was a job to free her. You couldn't move her, she was hung right up. There was a water-tight bulkhead you could open up from inside and then you could go in there with the beckets. You'd crawl right in there and pry and dig and get the buoy free. It was quite a job. Outside of that, considering those boats was runnin' every day, fog or anything, they did real well to stay out of trouble like they did.

We didn't steer too awful much—there were quartermasters who did most of that and threw the heaving line to get the lines ashore. If you was on your toes, you knew how to tighten up the lines just right so you didn't have to be tuggin' on any of them, which was good because there weren't no power winches like you'd have today. 'Course they had to line the ship up just right on the wharf.

I never had anything to do with runnin' the engine. The engineer did that. That was a whole different department. The *Morse* was a hard one for the fireman in the summertime. She was awful hot, and everything was hand work. She had a small fireroom, and on those hot, sticky summer days with no breeze, a lot of those firemen had to be dragged outa there—they'd passed out. She was a hard little devil to fire.

Oh, yeah, we put a long day in. Like I said, OSHA wouldn't approve of it. And another thing OSHA wouldn't have allowed either is I was only about sixteen when I was doin' this. The mate knew it, but all they wanted was a strong back and a weak mind. I had a little problem later on, when I was shipping out foreign. I had to get my papers changed over, because they said I was about three years older than I was supposed to be.

You'd be up anytime ha' past four or five o'clock, and when you left Rockland varied according to how much freight you had and how much came in on the Boston boat and what the tide was. You couldn't go into North Haven on low tides. You'd leave between five and seven in the morning—probably around six on the average—and get down to Bar Harbor. You'd lay there a couple of hours or so, and start back between 12:30 and 2. She'd go right along, at ten knots or better. Between landings you had a rest, unless you were the one balancing, but it was hard work.

We ran from Rockland to North Haven, Stoneton, Southwest, Northeast, Seal Harbor, Bar Harbor, and coming back, you might stop at Manset. We used to pick up a lot of fish at Manset. They'd box it up and ice it, and it'd be in Boston in the morning. If we got in on schedule, we'd have our freight out on the dock and we were usually done by seven. Sometimes, though, we'd pick up sardines in Bass Harbor—load her right up with sardines. There were occasions when the Boston boat would have to wait for us, and then the whole crew would go right across from one boat to the other. A hundred cans to a case, I think it was, and we'd get three or four thousand cases. We'd put five of those cases on a truck. It was quite a lot of runnin' back and forth.

The *Morse* burned coal. We wheeled it around in carts, held five hundred pounds. We had to wheel just so many of them every night when we come in. We'd clean out the freight, put the coal into bunkers, down manhole covers, cover them up again, hose the deck down and sweep it, and load what freight there was already on the wharf.

We'd have our supper after we left North Haven and be all finished by the time we got into Rockland. When we got done, we might go uptown and see a movie or something, or we might just stay on the boat.

We carried a lot of general freight—different vegetables, peas, and stuff. In the fall we'd pick up a lot of blueberries, all crated in wooden boxes. They'd bring the freight right down to the dock, and we'd put it on the Boston boat at night. She got in to Boston quite early. It was a good way to ship stuff.

With all those big estates down there on Mount Desert—the Rockefellers and the Fords and all—there was a lot of building then: all those big houses, bigger than hotels, on the side of the mountains. We used to lug a lot of water pipe, pieces that weighed six hundred pounds. Two of us, one on each end, on his shoulders, would lug it down. We used to say we probably sunk Mount Desert down about two feet with all the iron pipe we took over there.

We carried a lot of horses down in the spring and back in the fall. There were four bays going down through below—two in the middle where the engine was, and two on the outside, the wings. It was quite wide ahead of the paddlewheels, and they'd lead the horses in and put them in just like you were tying them up in a stall. They'd put them on the Boston boat, too, and take them back wherever they came from.

It was a nice way of traveling back then. Trucks done away with all that.

Steamship J. T. Morse.

COURTESY OF THE BOOTHBAY REGION HISTORICAL SOCIETY.

Lake Steamers and Other Boats

Arthur Hall
GREENVILLE · 1910S THROUGH 1930S

On Moosehead Lake there was a fleet of eight Coburn Company steamboats. It was a regular line, on schedules; they met trains and visited all those camps that took summer people, known as summer complaints. Each camp had its own little post office.

Just as soon as they put the highway in to Jackman, that all folded up.

A lot of people were guides in the summer, and they worked in the woods in the winter. There was a brisk time in the spring when the drive came down. All those steamers would be towing logs over to the sawmill or over to the Kennebec to go down the river to Skowhegan and the mills.

Ray Vigue
1940s

The Hollingsworth & Whitney [timber] Company owned the *Katahdin*, and I was responsible for the maintenance of that. They towed booms of logs and hauled supplies to various camps on Moosehead Lake, at Lily Bay, North Bay, Tomhegan, Rockwood, and Seboomook. Tons and tons of food, hay, grain, and tools.

Roy Monroe
MILO · 1910S AND 1920S

There are three rivers in Milo. One of them drains Sebec Lake—on the other side is Schoodic Lake, and up above that is Moosehead. They had old-fashioned steamboats. You could walk along the deck and look down into the engine room—it was about six feet square. The engine room was merely a recess, a little pocket in the deck of the steamboat. You'd walk by and if you stepped up six or seven inches from there, there was nothing but a rope strung through little rings to keep you from walking down into the engine room. You were midway up the engine, there. It was vertical; the pistons acted vertically, and the crankshaft was going in a fan-shaped motion right before your eyes. It was polished steel with steam coming out around it occasionally. All the fittings were brass and had to be oiled all the time—there was a man walking around in there every minute. It was low pressure—forty or fifty pounds, I would say—and it burned wood.

Steamship Katahdin, Moosehead Lake, beside her sister ship, which had sunk during the previous winter.
COURTESY OF RAY VIGUE.

On Sebec there were two or three steamboats. Sometime recently one of them was restored and used for a few years. Then they sank it, intentionally. I don't know why—people in Dover and Sebec do some very strange things, as everybody knows.

Roy Monroe on Other Boats

We had two motorboats. One my grandfather made, and when he got it all put together, he named it *Moneysunk*. It was one of the slowest boats in the world. It was about thirty feet long and had an engine from the Great Northern. It was a powerful thing, known as a make-and-break engine. They'd used it to pull log booms. It was frozen up, and he got it for little or nothing and had it welded up. Then he built the boat around it.

One time I borrowed my uncle's outboard, an Evinrude. It had a little wooden handle on the drum, and you took your hand and rotated it. Once it got to a certain place, it would start. Those two-cycle engines were very difficult to start unless you were used to them, and I wasn't. My friend had an oar he was using as a paddle. We went four miles, and we never did get it started. I took the plug off and turned it by hand so the propeller would turn, just for something to do. We only had the one oar, because we assumed the motor was going to run. Of course it did, the next day.

We had two canoes. My wife and I went on our honeymoon in a canoe.

Gertrude Fraser
Verona · 1920s

In Malden, there was a man who delivered milk and one who delivered bread and others who delivered everything, using horses. The milkman's horse knew the route. He'd leave the horse and cut through backyards, and the horse would meet him there at the next stop. But they didn't deliver anything on the island here. Every day we used to walk through the woods to the next farm to get our milk, and we used to go up to Bucksport in the motorboat to get our groceries. Sometimes we'd row. We'd go when the tide was right, coming in, and row home when it was going out.

The motorboat we got later was probably about twenty feet and had a one-lunger engine. Aunt Sadie was deaf, but for some reason, if you put her in that motorboat and talked to her, she could hear you.

Isabel Ames
Northport · 1910s

My father was a fisherman, and his boat was a salmon-wherry type. Ever since I was big enough to sit up, I've been able to row. He always used to take us out to the salmon nets. And if my mother didn't know what we were going to have for supper, she'd tell us to go catch a fish. You could go out there anytime and catch a haddock or a flounder. I don't think there's a fish in the bay now.

My father used to walk to Masons' meetings, and if they visited another chapter, someone would take a horse and wagon. There was no ferry to Islesboro at that time. The men used to go over and visit the Masonic Lodge over there. Either someone had to have a boat, or they'd find one to take them over. Uncle Orren had a boat. He was a boatbuilder, in fact, and he used to carry produce and sometimes passengers over to Dark Harbor. Once he took our family to the island. I don't remember what the occasion was, whether it was a picnic or just a trip or what. His boat was all enclosed. It sat five or six on benches along the side. I don't remember much about the motor. Machinery and I don't get along very well, so that didn't interest me. I've never driven a car. I'm still bumming rides. But I'm not one who thinks she has to be going places all the time.

Captain Bill Abbott
VERONA • 1920s AND 1930s

My father used to tow salmon. The fish hatchery up in Orland would buy salmon off the weir fishermen, and he would take them up there with a twenty-two-foot boat that he and his friend Frank Bennett built. They put the fish in dories with the sides cut out and wire over them. He'd tow the dories over to where the locks were, and someone else would tow them to the Alamoosook fish hatchery. He used to take people to dances in that boat, too. There was a dance hall at the foot of Verona.

Arthur Hall
1920s

I went with Uncle Will summers, after he retired. He agreed with Dr. Johnson that sailing was like being in jail with the additional hazard of being drowned. It was a hard way to make a living, but he was addicted to it. Even retired, he had to have some kind of a boat, so he went to Winchenbach's yard in Christmas Cove and asked, "You got that sardine carrier model?" "Yes, I do." "Could I take it back and modify it a little?" So he did that. It was during Depression time, so Uncle Will told Winchenbach that when there wasn't work for his crew, to work on the sardine carrier, and when there was, to lay her up.

She was a short ketch rig, gaff-headed. I felt completely safe and secure with him, because he knew the coast like the back of his hand. Even in the fog, he'd keep going. He'd take a bearing on a bell or a lighthouse or something, and I'd steer. I liked to steer, and he didn't. He'd say, "Bring her over, boy," and I'd bring her over; he'd say, "Let it be so," and I'd let it be so. I'd have a great big compass under my nose, and I'd steer all day. We'd come into a harbor somewhere and find all kinds of yachts inside—they hadn't dared to go out. He'd tell them, "Look, it's clear as daylight outside, I'll lead you out," but no one would follow him.

He really knew that coast. It was a wonderful education to sail with him.

One time, thick-a-fog, he decided to go into the mouth of the Kennebec. There was a Coast Guard station there at that time. Elmer Crowley, his nephew, was the head of it. They were all related along the coast, in those days. We came out of the fog, and there was the Coast Guard station—and there on the dock was Elmer Crowley. "That's about the closest landfall I ever made," said Uncle Will.

The old man used to get up early, and he'd say, "Get outa that bunk or I'll use a barrel stave on you." He'd have you out at daylight in the 'pod, scrubbing topsides. You didn't eat much during the day, because you were underway—pilot bread or a donut or two—but we'd put in pretty early.

Sometimes he'd say it was about time for a fry. His tender was a peapod, and we'd take the 'pod in to the flats at low tide, with a clam rake. I was a young, strong boy, and I'd dig the clams and get cramps in my legs from bending over. Finally he couldn't stand it anymore, and he'd say, "Give me that rake." All of a sudden the clams would come out like buckshot. We'd take them aboard and cook them on that fisherman stove and eat those clams till we bulged and went to sleep.

In the center of the harbor at Matinicus, there was a lobster car ten by forty feet, and we used to make fast to that. One time he told me, "There's a blow coming, and I think we'll go out and see how she'll lie to." Sure enough, he headed straight out to sea, and it started to blow. He took in sail and reefed the main and hove to; all of a sudden the boat was calm. We went below and had a dinner of fried clams. We were as comfortable as if we were in an old rocking chair. I did notice the old gent go up the steps and poke his light around and see if there was any chafe, and then we went to bed. A couple of days later, it was all over, and he said, "Yup, she'll lie to."

I was out in Addison one time, and I decided to go out with Frankie Reynolds in his new lobsterboat. He was going to start out before daylight, so he said, "You put a length of cordline around your big toe and hang it out the window." I did that, and went to sleep. When all of a sudden my big toe about fell off, I knew it was time, so I got up and went with him. It was thick-a-fog, and we went out. I had no idea where we were. Once or twice we had the stern almost on the ledges. The lobster bait was pretty ripe and there was a long hard swell, but I didn't get seasick.

When I went with Uncle Will, he asked me if I got seasick, and I said no. "You know what that means?" he asked me. "It just means you haven't been to sea much."

But I went on the Bermuda race in 1932 in a big sloop, and it was pretty rough and blowing hard. All the crew except me were experienced ocean racers, and they all were seasick. I wasn't. But when we got into Bermuda, into Hamilton Harbour, I walked up the steps coming from the water. Suddenly, when I got onto level ground, I had to go behind some bushes, and I threw everything up. So I've never been seasick, but I was landsick.

Uncle Will and Aunt Net lived together in South Portland until they were ninety-six or ninety-seven. One time I asked him, "Uncle Will, how do you keep so active?"

"Well, boy, I never stop."

Remembering Stonington

Jim Greenlaw

Jim Greenlaw.
PHOTO BY VIRGINIA L. THORNDIKE.

When I was three, my mother died in the flu epidemic. There were five of us kids, and my father was a stonecutter who had to be away a lot of the time. A quarry would get a job, and then it might be inactive for a while, so the stonecutters had to go where the jobs were. He worked in New Hampshire and Vermont and Canada—all over the Northeast. My family was split up. I went to Stonington to live with an aunt and uncle. My uncle was sixty-four years old when I came. He and my Aunt Lil had never had any children of their own. Maybe that's why they took me on, but it must've been something at his age.

He was one of the best fathers you could ever have.

He was born in 1856, and I got a lot of history from him. When he was fourteen, he went to Springfield, Missouri. He had a brother out there in business, making wagons and selling grain and coal. My uncle stayed in Springfield for ten years, till he was twenty-four, and then spent the rest of his life in Stonington. Oceanville and South Deer Isle were the business parts of town at first, though you wouldn't think so today. What built up Stonington was the quarries. The quarry business here is not too old, but once it opened, it boomed. The stone's beautiful, and it's easy to work, too.

Uncle John and his brother ran a country grocery store on the waterfront. All stores was on the waterfront—everything came by steamboat. Well, in Uncle John's day, it was packets—small sailing vessels. The news of Lincoln's assassination came by packet either two or three days after it happened. Uncle John was nine years old then.

Growing up here on Deer Isle, our only connection was to Rockland and Swans Island. We had a ferry of a sort, a scow towed by a lobsterboat. The first one I remember carried two or three cars, Model Ts. There were very few of those. There was two odd-ball Model Ts remade into a sort of a snowmobile,

The car ferry to Deer Isle was not the steamer in the background of this photo but the simple scow in the foreground, with one vehicle already loaded.
COURTESY OF BROOKSVILLE HISTORICAL SOCIETY.

you'd call it, with a track on back, skis on front. The doctor had one, and the mail carrier had one. There weren't very many cars; it was mostly horses until after I was five or six years old.

Later, they built bigger scows, carried maybe six cars. Then there were two of them, one coming and one going all the time. They did the best they could to carry the traffic. If there was something like the Blue Hill Fair going on, it was all right going over because they spread out. But they'd come back in a bunch, and you'd be waiting for hours. Ordinarily they'd lay up for a while at night, but if somebody was sick, if there was an emergency, they'd take them across whenever it was.

Winters, nobody used cars, except those snowmobile things, and they didn't work so good. People didn't try to plow the snow, they let it build up. Our house in Stonington was on a bank, with steps down to the road—twelve or thirteen of them. I used to keep track of how deep the snow was; some years it was two or three steps. Then when it started to break up, there was a slush problem. But drainage was good; it just went overboard.

They did go on the ice with the Model Ts—it was quite common to go across the Reach with them. It's not very far across there—one of the first places to freeze up. There are several cars on the bottom there, too, though.

There must have been times when you couldn't get across the Reach at all. If you only had two or three inches of ice and it wasn't cold enough to freeze any more, but it was too hard to break up, there might be a while when you couldn't cross. My memory's kind of vague. I do remember that an elderly man up to Little Deer Isle who carried mail back and forth used to brag he'd never missed a day. He used to row. Somehow he'd get across—either he'd take an oar and break the ice or he'd walk.

The boats to Swans Island and Rockland would run year-round. It was interesting, those old steamboats breaking through the ice. The harbor in Stonington and sometimes the whole bay froze up. One of the big events was when the boat couldn't get in to the wharf. Sometimes the ice would be a foot and a half or two feet thick, and it was something to see the boat breaking through it. Instead of running up onto it and breaking it, they just had to powerfully break into it. It was awfully hard on the boats. They would break through the ice as close as they could get to Stonington—sometimes a mile off—and unload everything onto the ice. They'd come out and pick it up with horse teams and sleds. But hardly ever did they miss a trip. They took mail delivery serious in those days.

It's unusual, but they have driven cars to Isle au Haut. It wouldn't be across

Mail boat at Keller's Point, Islesboro.

COURTESY OF THE ISLESBORO HISTORICAL SOCIETY.

Steamship Mount Desert *sailing past Crotch Island, Stonington.*

Frank Claes Collection.

an open area. There's a lot of islands out there, and they'd go from one to another. It's six miles altogether.

As I look back, it seems as though it was the usual thing at least for the harbor to freeze up. If you had a motorboat, it was small. Most fishing boats were sloops, single-masted sailboats. They weren't boats that could keep the harbor clear. There must have been mild winters when it didn't freeze up, but my memory is that most every winter, the harbor froze up.

There are ways of getting across ice that's shaky. One way was skis, to spread your weight out. Kidlike, as soon's the ice began to make in the harbor, we couldn't wait to get on it. Uncle John always encouraged us to wait till it was good and solid, and even then to take something with you in case you broke through—skis or a pole to hold onto till somebody could come get you.

Saltwater ice is tricky. It takes more of it to hold you up, but living right beside it, we got pretty wise. Most times it wasn't a dangerous thing. I don't remember any bad incidents. Most times we were around the shore jumping ice cakes—a good many of us got wet that way—but we were pretty careful.

If it was necessary to go somewhere on the ice, they had tiny boats, light like a canoe. You could drag them behind you, and then you had a boat if you needed one.

When the ice wasn't bad, you could go to Rockland on the steamer and come back in a day. That's where you did your shopping. The boat would spend the night in Swans Island after touching here at four in the afternoon, and then in the morning she'd get back to Stonington. You'd get aboard at five in the morning, and in a couple of hours you'd be in Rockland. You'd spend the day there, and then at one thirty or two you'd get aboard again and come home. I think it was the *Vinalhaven*, first—there was the *Vinalhaven*, the *North Haven*, the *Bardwell*, the *White*, and several more.

The steamer comin' in was the social part of the evening. When the boat came through the Thorofare, she'd blow the whistle, and then it would take about an hour to get the mail to the post office and get it sorted. Everyone would go downstreet to the post office, 'specially the kids. It was unsupervised time for us—we could get together with our friends. It was so hectic with all the crowds, usually, they'd lock the post office, and then they'd try to let you in easy. In the winter, it was after dark, and that made it all the more interesting, because you could meet your girlfriends downtown.

We went to Rockland quite often. Uncle John's doctor was there, and I remember going over with him. I

HOW WE GOT THERE FROM HERE

couldn't have been more than five or six years old, but I remember one thing in particular. Uncle John had heart problems and had trouble walking. I was worried to death about him. The doctor saw I was so concerned, and he said, "I'll give you a job to do. Twice a day, you take his pulse and keep a record." I did that for a long time. I don't know that it made any difference, really, but it made me feel better to have that job.

It was a short walk to the doctor, but if my uncle didn't feel well, we'd take a taxi. Rockland had more cars than we had. That was one of the fun things about it—there was quite a lot of traffic.

The steamers were stinky. They ran on coal, and when you came aboard on the lower deck, you got a lot of coal fumes and noise and smoke and heat.

Then you went up to the saloon, they called it, and it was kinda nice. It was finished off in red plush, and there were lots of windows that you could open or close according to the weather. You could go out on deck and feel the wind on your face. It was beautiful—at least I loved it.

And then there was the Boston boat. I only made one trip, when I was twelve years old. I'd just graduated from grammar school. One of my brothers was living with an aunt in Ipswich, Massachusetts, and she asked all of us kids to come up and spend a little time with them. Two sisters and a brother and I all went on the Boston boat; I don't remember if it was the *Camden* or the *Belfast*. They were both great. They were big and fancy, and the best part of it was you left here at five in the morning, and you could be in Boston that night. Well, it might have been after midnight, but that night sometime.

The mail delivery up here, and most places on the island, was done with a horse and carriage. That was also my way of getting transportation. Some of my brothers and sisters still lived in Oceanville, and I visited whenever I could. Anybody could hitch a ride with the mail carrier. I think they'd charge you a quarter. It was no big deal to walk, either—it's four miles to Stonington from here. But when I was small, they probably insisted I come up with the mail team. That's what they called it, the mail team. It was a single horse and an ordinary wagon with some kind of a shelter over the front seat—my memory's pretty vague. It wasn't a big rig. It didn't have to be—there might have been a couple of gunnysack-size bags of mail.

There were oxen, too. One family in particular that lived down in Stonington, the Ames family, had oxen, way back as far as I can remember. They were beauties, too. A lot of them did road work. They were strong, and you could load them down heavy. People did plowing with them, and this family run a little quarry—cut cellar stone. Before they opened that quarry, a lot of the cellar stone on the island came from Blue Hill. My uncle talked about taking cellar stone from

Fred Eaton driving the mail carrier on Deer Isle in 1907. The vehicle was painted red, white, and blue.
FRANK CLAES COLLECTION.

Oxen pulling a load of hay.
Courtesy of Lincolnville Historical Society.

Blue Hill with ox teams, loading it onto vessels, bringing it in as close as they could, and unloading it and taking it up where it was going. A lot of work.

Oxen are steady, where horses get frightened. I scared a horse one time. There was a hitching post at the store my two uncles run, and when I got out of school, I'd run down the alley and jump on the platform. This one day, I went on with a thump, and there was a skittish horse tied there. He took off, and you know something? I did, too. I don't know if anyone knew I did it, but I didn't stop to find out. He left the wagon right there.

There were a lot of schooners and lobsterboats then. Most of the lobsterboats were sloop boats. I've often thought that those guys must've been awful clever to haul lobster traps in a sailboat, coming into the wind and hauling a trap. They must have been expert.

They had barges, that's how they transported stone. A lot of those barges were just sailing ships cut down, towed by a tugboat. Some of them were monstrous—three- or four-masters stripped down. They'd be filled with stone and towed to Boston or New York or wherever. I can remember times when there'd be three and four of those waiting to be loaded.

Occasionally it was a bit dangerous on the water with the barges. They had no power, and there were times when the tug had to cut one loose, if a storm blew up or if a barge got a bad leak they couldn't stop. When I was real young, this happened once, and the crew came to my aunt and uncle's inn for the night, I don't remember if there were three or four men, but in the excitement of getting off the barge and onto the tug, they forgot the dog, locked in the cabin. They could hear him barking as they left, and they couldn't go back for him. They were very sad men over dinner.

There were two big quarries on Crotch Island, one big one on St. Helena, and numerous little ones on almost all the small islands. Paving motions, they were called. Most of those were run by two men, and all they did was break out paving stones for city streets. If you've been in old cities and seen the old cobblestones, chances are they came from this area.

They carried pulpwood in little schooners, and they used to bring our firewood, too. There wasn't enough wood on the island to supply our stoves, so wood and coal used to be big business. Coal sometimes came on barges, towed in by steam tugboats. The first one I remember was the *Betsy Ross*. Next was the *Eugenie Spofford*. She was owned by the John L. Goss quarry, and I think the *Betsy* was too. Even if a big tugboat came in to pick up a barge, the quarry had to have one to bring it into the wharf.

The biggest thrill I ever got was the first day I saw a seaplane. It circled around and landed and came into the wharf. I was four or five years old. Nobody came up with the money to let me go up in it, but a few years later, they used to come in and land on the pond. I was eleven or twelve by then, and I used to go up with them. Wasn't that a thrill! You probably weren't up ten or fifteen minutes at the most, but that was a big event. Somebody from Rockland would come in every winter with a plane with skis, usually on Sundays. On good days you could almost depend on him coming. He used to make a good living at it. I think it cost a couple of dollars to go up, a lot of money at that time. He took two passengers at a time.

My uncles had a horse to deliver groceries. That was another fun thing I did as a kid—rode with my uncle when he delivered groceries. You might go out two or three times in a day. You might be out a couple of hours in the morning, and then if somebody called in an order you'd take it, even if it was just one order.

There was one road, just a tiny road, with two houses in there. One of them was a regular stop. An elderly woman lived there, taking care of her crippled sister. They had no way to get out, so we used to deliver all their groceries to them. Now I deliver groceries in there from the local food pantry, and my daughter goes with me. "You know something?" I said to her, "I used to deliver groceries when I was five or six years old, and here I am seventy-five years later doing the same damn thing. Same road, same house. I haven't advanced very far in all those years."

Snow

Rena Bunker
TURNER • 1910s

Summers, there was a fellow who rented horses—there were a lot of people who liked to ride in the summer, I guess—and he didn't know what to do with his horses in the winter. I took one. My father didn't want anything to do with it, so I took care of it, fed it, and cleaned its stall out and everything. He didn't touch it. Sometimes I rode horseback to school and towed my brother on skis. We skied a lot of places and went on snowshoes. We had an awful lot of snow in those days.

We had one of those sleighs with two seats. They called them pungs, and I used to go back and forth to school in it. A pung wasn't all fancied up like some sleighs—you set on the hard board seat and froze to death. The horse would have icicles all over him. There was a barn near the school, and I kept my horse in there. Another fellow did, too. I was always full of the devil—one time I hid his harness on him. Of course he knew who did it, and the next time I went for my horse, the pung was up in the rafters. I had to ride home bareback. "What happened to the pung?" my father wanted to know.

"It's up the top of the barn," I told him, and I told him how it got there.

He called the boy's father. "You tell your son to leave my daughter alone," he said.

"Well, you tell her to leave my boy alone!" the man said. "She didn't tell you the rest of the story, did she?"

Horse and sleigh.
COURTESY OF THE LINCOLN COUNTY HISTORICAL ASSOCIATION.

They didn't have snowplows and things then. They had these great big wooden rollers drawn by four or six horses. That just packed the snow down so hard they could go on it. That was before cars. I don't remember what they did when they first had cars.

They don't have snow like they used to.

Snow roller drawn by four pairs of horses, junction of Cedar and Main Streets, Belfast.
COURTESY OF DORIS HALL.

Bessie Dean
LINCOLNVILLE · 1920s

You know how they used to break out the roads after a snowstorm? They'd have a horse and a sled and a big heavy chain, which they'd loop right around the back and drag it behind. That's what they called breaking out the roads. Fletcher Martin used to do it on the road where we lived.

Roy Monroe
MILO · 1910s AND 1920s

Sliding was a way of life with kids in Milo. There was one whole street that was set aside in winter. There was no sand put on it. The kids had it.

I had a kick sled—a Scandinavian invention with long J-shaped runners that looked like soup ladles but had quarter-inch steel in the front. The two were set parallel to each other, two feet apart, and there was a wooden seat and two handles on either side of a crossbar. You'd set yourself on it and balance one foot on one side of the steel runners, and to turn, you'd turn the handle, and the steel would push against your foot and bring you around. Downhill, you could go like blazes. One day I did, down into the square here. I got onto some ice, and it took my feet; made me an unwilling passenger with my feet behind me, my belly almost on the ground.

I didn't use it for a while after that.

My grandfather almost developed something. He took a conventional sled with steel runners, then he added bicycle pedals and geared them up and used a thing like a sprocket that dug into the ice and dragged you along. You pedaled with your feet and steered with your hands.

Doris Hall
BELFAST · 1910s

I can remember when I was in sixth grade there was a snowstorm, and my father came down to walk me home from school. I was so ashamed! To think my father would come to meet me. I had quite a little distance to go, and he thought it would be better if he came and got me.

That winter, of course, everybody shoveled their own sidewalks. You took it for granted—the City Council didn't have to tell you. The snow was piled up so high you could not see a team going by in the road. You could only hear the bells. I can remember what fun it was to listen to the tinkling of those bells. That snow lasted nearly all winter long; it never melted off. When it snowed, it snowed on top.

We had an awful lot of snow when I was a youngster, and the teams would go over it. There were no automobiles in the winter, and there were probably not

Main Street in Belfast, 1912.
COURTESY OF DORIS HALL.

more than four or five people in town that had one anyway. They used to have a snow roller—I think I saw it once. I know I'd hear my father speaking about it.

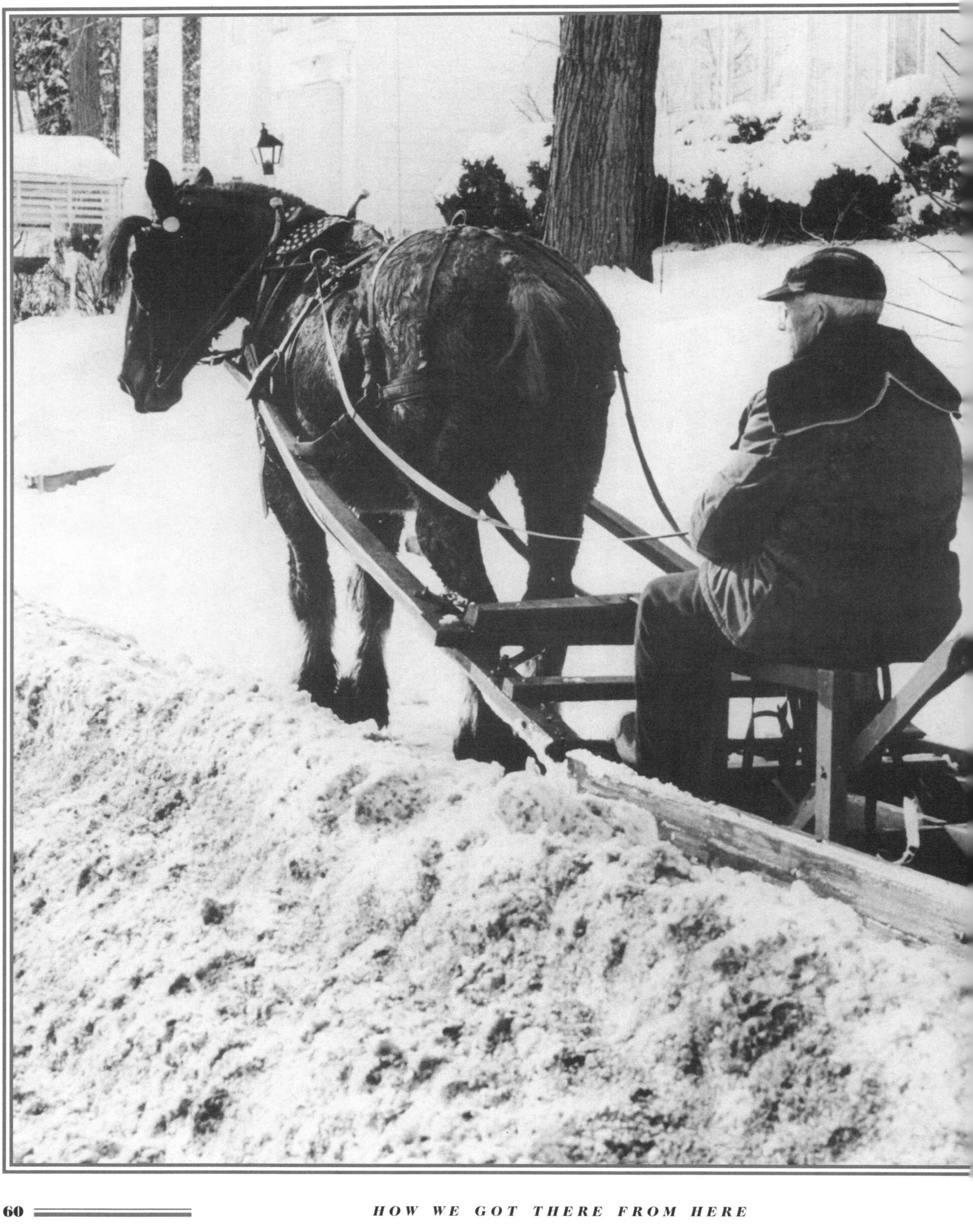

But at that time, I wasn't curious about it.

Oh, boy, how we dressed! We had long pants—we called them drawers—and I can see them now. I've never forgiven them. They were awful. In the winter, they'd be hung on the line, and you'd bring those things in, and they'd drip on the kitchen floor—you'd have to dry them out. We all wore hats in those days, and we were bundled up in scarves and mittens and all that.

The first man who put skis on the front wheels of his automobile was a doctor. There were not many people who used a car in the wintertime—there weren't too many people who had cars anyway—but he wanted it to help him get around, so he put skis on the front. The snow would get packed down so hard it would be slippery, and he would have a hard time maneuvering that car. We kids would slide down Court Street, in front of his house, and he'd be driving along Cedar Street. He'd see us kids coming—he was doing his best to manage the automobile and we didn't help. I don't know but that's when he took up swearing.

Went Durkee
ISLESBORO • 1930s

First snowplow we had on the island, it was called a dustpan 'cause it looked like one. It was so heavy one truck couldn't push it, so they got a mooring pole, hitched it onto another truck, and the two of them pushed it. Didn't matter about ditches—when the first truck went into a ditch, the second one pulled him out.

Plowing the sidewalk, Kennebunk, 1919.

COURTESY OF THE MAINE DEPARTMENT OF TRANSPORTATION.

Raymond Oxton and Old Harry

Raymond Oxton.
PHOTO BY VIRGINIA L. THORNDIKE.

LINCOLNVILLE

When I was a kid growin' up, if you wanted to go to Camden in the wintertime, you either took an old horse or you walked. That was before electric lights. I been here since I was seven months old—it'd have to take me that long to make such a mess. I was born three and a half miles from here—the poor old doctor came up from Camden with a horse and officiated. He said, "By gorry, he looks like a little monkey, all wizzled up."

My father said, "He'll never live," but I'm still here. I'm eighty-four.

From the day Mother got married to the day she landed here, she'd moved nineteen times. She was taking in washings, nothing but old-fashioned scrub boards, two tubs, heatin' water on the stove, ironing by kerosene lamp. But she kept us kids fed. My father enjoyed liquid refreshment more than anything else. There was four kids: Roy, Arthur, my sister, Bernice, and me.

In the early twenties, from December to April, there was no cars goin' by here. The mail came with a team of horses. Frank Pendleton had a pair of mules north of the beach, up where Tommy Flagg lives now, and Leon Barton had a pair up in Northport.

The roads wasn't plowed or anything. They used to drag a chain behind the horse sleds to kinda keep the hummocks down. I went to Camden one time to go to a movie; they were playing *Iron Horse*. I was down there three days. There was a storm, and no traffic—no horses, no nothin'—went through for three days. They finally came down with a horse and a pung sled with a box on it, and that's where the mailman and I rode.

There used to be an old big barn at the top of Spring Brook Hill, this side, on the lower side of the road. They used to leave the horses in there, and the mailman would take his mailbag on his back and snowshoe on into Camden.

Mud season? Oh, my God. Good gorry, yes. You were lucky to get through with a horse. The McLaughlin Brothers were the first ones to put on a bus—an old big Buick, seven passenger, I guess. They used to carry a chain, and if one could get through, it could pull another one through. They used to carry loads of hay and brush to get 'em up out of the mud.

The McLaughlin Brothers were the first ones to plow the Number One highway. The first time they come down through, they had three Cleveland tractors with a V-plow, a built-up plank V-plow. There was one with the plow, one behind pushin', and one ahead, pullin'. They was in the road, in the ditch, everywhere. They hired Great Northern Paper Company to open it up in the

A pung loaded with wood.

COURTESY OF LINCOLNVILLE HISTORICAL SOCIETY.

springtime. They had three crews on foot—one down on the roadbed, throwin' it up as far as they could, and another one on the top of each bank, throwin' it back, all by hand.

I've gone to Camden with a pair of horses, before they changed the telephone lines, and I been settin' on the sled and reached out and touched the wires. We were on twelve or fourteen feet of snow. They used to go way back of that house, up through the fields and in back of the white house, just to get around that snow.

I used to go down in the morning and shovel a path into the school and build a fire in an old box stove, for twenty-five cents a week. The high school was in Camden. When we got ready to go to high school, 'course there wasn't no school bus. You wanted to go to high school, you had to either walk down or catch a ride with someone. The first two years I rode with Lloyd Pitcher from just north of the beach—he had an old Model T. Or sometimes I went with Arwilda Ames from Northport. Then my third year, I bought an old Chevy, and I carried kids for $1.25 a week. That paid—back in those days you could get seven gallons of gas for a dollar. The first car was an old touring car, with side curtains on it. With all the kids, it shortened up; it had mechanical brakes, and I'd have to adjust them. Then if I happened to be alone, it'd stretch out again. I had to reline the brakes on that thing three times a year.

When I got out of school—1931—I had no job, but I had a few cows. I told Mother, we won't make anything but maybe we'll make a living. There's gonna be people coming here summers, and they're gonna need milk. I started off milking by hand and finally got a Surge milker. I started delivering milk on a bicycle with a basket on the back. I did that for about three years. I had a twelve-quart crate on the back and side carriers—oh, I might possibly have carried twenty quarts. In the winter, I took a hand sled and put the rope over my shoulders. I took three twenty-four-quart carriers from the Northport line to the Camden line, every day. I bottled it myself.

It's hard to imagine now, but you used to be able to sit right here and look out the window and see the Boston boat come around the point up there. If you had a good horse and you had anything you wanted to put on the steamer, you'd head that poor horse to Camden and meet the boat. I had strawberries or a veal calf once in a while.

I can remember the bay freezing over, twice. When I was a little fellow, there was a barge out here, half or two-thirds of the way across, froze into the ice. Folks walked across to it. And one time, my uncle took a hand sled and a boat and left the Lobster Pound and went across to Seven Hundred Acre Island. When he got to the channel where the boats went up through, he took the boat and rowed across.

They used to haul hay across to the island from Belfast. That I did not see. But we were heating with wood back then, and I can remember one winter we had a period of two weeks when the thermometer never went above twenty-five below zero, day or night. Now we complain when it gets down to zero.

Fred Hardy, down on Fernalds Neck, he had an old black horse. I had a few people with woodlots wanted wood hauled out. I don't know how I happened to talk with Fred, but he said, "Take old Harry down and keep him." When I first had him, you'd hitch him onto a sled and by the time you'd walked up to Pitcher Pond, where my brother had a woodlot, he'd be all white with sweat. You'd put on a few small logs, and that was enough. But I got him hardened up so he could take a good load. One time I was coming down the road off the mountain and there was a man working in there with a pair of horses. "Where's your other horse?" he asked me.

"Dunno. Why?"

"You got any idea how much wood you got on?"

I had nine feet of mountain wood on—that's a foot over a cord. When I got back on the mountain, I cut the stakes right in half. My brother wanted to know why I did that. "Just 'cause that horse is willing to haul all that is no reason to kill him over it," I said.

Turned out that horse was twenty-six years old. He knew more about working in the woods than I'll ever know. You'd hitch him up the first time and take him down to the landing; the next time, you'd just hitch him up and send him out. He'd come out right where you took him the first time. You could unload him and send him back.

But he was a windsucker. You know, where they put their teeth over a board and suck in air. When you started out—*fffttt, fffttt, fffttt*—you'd be all the way to Ducktrap before you got the wind out of him.

If he fell down in the snow, he would not move until you told him to. He'd stay quiet, and you'd say, "Try it, Harry," and he'd try it. Kept himself out of trouble. But if a truck went by with a piece of canvas flipping, he'd jump and tangle his feet up and go head over teakettle, all hitched in with the sled and everything. I'd always go help him get untangled, but one time my brother was there. He'd had horses a long time, before, and he just hollered, "Come on, Harry!" and the old horse got right on his feet. But if you tried to back that horse up with a load, he'd almost set down. His back had been hurt sometime along, but he'd do what you asked him to, no matter how much it hurt.

Horses

Albert Chatfield
ROCKPORT • 1910s

This area had rather few tourists when I was a boy, and not many tourist accommodations. Before the automobile, you have to remember, people were dependent upon horses to a very large extent. The gallery down in Rockport started life as a livery stable. Livery stables were essential. A lot of people wanted their own horse and buggy, but the last thing they wanted was to have to maintain a horse. So there were livery stables—seven in Camden, at one time. The one in Rockport had two floors of horses below street level, and the stable boy who brought the horse up and harnessed it would drive to the house and then walk back. A lot of houses had carriage houses; they'd have no horse there, but they'd have the carriage house.

Fine horse and buggy, Islesboro.
COURTESY OF THE ISLESBORO HISTORICAL SOCIETY.

Peg Miller
LINCOLNVILLE • 1920s AND 1930s

Father had a top buggy—a riding wagon with a folding top on it. If you had a top buggy, it was supposed to mean you had a little money, but that wasn't so. Sometimes the farmers would horse-trade until they got one. It mustn't have been too expensive, or my father wouldn't have had one. We were poor. It was neat, though—they're up high, you know. If you're not used to high altitudes, you might not like it.

The wheels were big, so you could get through the muck and mire. It had four wheels, but they were right close together. There was just one seat—you could get two kids and an adult on it. There was a little place in the rear end of it where you could put something under the seat if you wanted to. We always had a horse blanket that you put over your lap. If it was cold, that felt good, let me tell you. Sometimes the horse would trot a little bit—not like a riding horse, this was just a workhorse. But it'd kinda splash—you were quite close. And then if you had to wait someplace and the horse had to stand, you'd put it over him, 'cause he'd be hot.

Nobody had riding horses then. You had to make that hay pay.

When I was in high school, there was no transportation. The first three years, I went to Searsport and stayed with one of my brothers over there. I worked my way—he had small children, and I learned how to take care of babies. The fourth year, they moved into Northport to be on a paved road, and I went to Belfast. Robert A. Hall used to go to Belfast for high school—he lived down on Slab City Road—so I got to ride with him in his car for two dollars a week. There was another car going back and forth, but it was filled. The boys used to walk to Belfast. My husband did that until his last year, when he got a car. Lee Thurlow worked in Belfast at the Sash and Blind, and if the boys got out on the road in time, he'd pick them up and take them in. He'd fill the car right up. Then they'd walk home—there weren't too many people driving by, that time of day. They couldn't do any sports or anything. They had to get home to help on the farm.

That's why so many people my age didn't have a high-school education.

Mainly my father used the top buggy to take me to Hall's to go to school. But sometimes, when the traveling was real bad, we'd go somewhere else or even to Belfast to get a bag of grain. You could put a bag of grain in the rear—just barely—but a bag of grain went a long way in those days, because you didn't have much stock.

I always say, anyone that hasn't ridden in a horse and buggy—or gone on a surrey with a fringe on top, or been to a one-room school, or used an outhouse—hasn't lived.

Surry with a fringe on top.
COURTESY OF THE UNION HISTORICAL SOCIETY.

Albert Chatfield

We had a pair of English coach horses, and they pulled a big buckboard—an open wagon with three seats across it. The coachman sat up on a high seat in front. We would have elaborate picnics in places like the top of Mount Battie. The

Picnickers in a buckboard on Mount Desert Island.

COURTESY OF THE MAINE HISTORIC PRESERVATION COMMISSION.

whole family would go, and relatives and guests; a lot of people imported their own friends from other cities. I remember a friend of my father's, Eugene F. Bliss, who ran a school in Cincinnati—he was a Harvard graduate back in the fifties. He lived until 1917. He used to come and spend a month or six weeks with us.

Whole groups of us would go out on outings. We provided our own entertainment in those days. That was the difference.

Rena Bunker
TURNER · 1910s

I remember my grandfather—he was a minister—had a surrey, and a trotting horse. He'd go up and down the coast and have a service somewhere each day. Then he'd be back for the service in Pembroke on Sunday.

Nettie Douglas
DEER ISLE · 1910s

Uncle Mel had the mail. One time when the Reach froze over, he brought the mail over from Sargentville and got back at half-past eleven at night. There was a great big snowbank, and the horse had to go through it. He threw himself, so Uncle Mel come back on his feet with the mail. The least little thing, I'd wake up, so I came down to help him sort. Then he went out delivering and met the old horse halfway in—he'd got himself up. Uncle Mel had to take him back to the barn, wash him up, cover him up, and put his blanket on—he was all sweaty. It was one o'clock when we got done with the mail.

Raymond Pendleton
ISLESBORO · 1910S

My grandfather, Captain Ed, used to sail on those four-masted schooners all over the world. He was retired when I was a kid. He took my father to sea one trip, trying to make him into a sailor, but my father wouldn't buy it.

My grandfather liked racehorses. When I was a youngster, my father and I would go over to the island, and he'd come down with his buckboard to get us. They used to have hills out there, just like here on the mainland. They've cut them all down today, but then they were steep. When we got to one of those hills, my father and I had to get out and walk, because the racehorse couldn't carry us all—it was too much work.

Everybody knew my grandfather had that racehorse and a light buggy—I rode with him once and found out about it. Another buggy started to go by, but he didn't make it. When the other horse came alongside, that racehorse just took off by himself. My grandfather cheered him on. We went pretty fast!

Isabel Ames
NORTHPORT · 1900S AND 1910S

We always had a horse and wagon, sometimes a pair of horses. They were regular farm horses—not draft horses, but not fancy carriage horses either. Father had what we called a grocery wagon—it was two-seated—and in the winter, he had what we called a pung. It had two seats, too. My father drove the school team—someone who had a horse and wagon would take the kids to school. There were four of us down this way.

He'd take the horse and wagon to town shopping, but we didn't have to buy much. We always did our own plowing and haying, and we raised most of our own food. We just had to go to town for staples, and Father used to ship apples and eggs. I remember in the winter he would be cleaning and packing apples and taking them to the Boston boat. In summer, of course, he used to meet the Boston boat and furnish transportation for some of the summer people. He'd pick them up and take them away in the fall, too.

One time I thought I'd like to try riding horseback. I found an old saddle in the barn, and I got the horse out and put the saddle on him. I rode up the road and down again, and when I got back, I no longer had the blanket—I don't know what happened to it. I guess I put the saddle on wrong. I felt as if I was on top of the Empire State Building—it's the same sensation as I have in a plane now: "My, that's a long way down there, and nothing in between!" I bet that horse thought he was going through some strange experience—but he didn't dump me, anyway. That was before my sister Alwilda was born. I couldn't have been more than eight.

Went Durkee
ISLESBORO · 1920S

When their stables were going full blast, Lester Hale and Tom Pendleton had eighteen or twenty men apiece drivin' surreys. Linwood Pendleton—they called him Goomer—had a one-horse stable, with a single-seat wagon. If he had two passengers, he'd walk. But at that time, a lot of people owned land on both sides of the road, and they'd run a gate across the road so their cattle could go out to pasture and come back into the barn. My father always walked and led the horses—he said he wouldn't have time to get up and down off the wagon to open all the gates.

The Catholics used to get up at five in the morning to go to church. I used to get up at three to feed the horses. I'll say that for the Catholics, they go to church. I've been down there by the church when there were so many horses you couldn't speak to your horse or they'd all go. You had to just touch him easy on the rump to start him up.

The first picnic I went on was in a hay rack. We went from Dark Harbor School to Sprague's Beach. Now, I tell you, that's a long way to go with an old pair

Austin Lewis driving children to school, late 1930s.
COURTESY OF THE BOOTHBAY REGION HISTORICAL SOCIETY.

Horse and hay rack.

COURTESY OF THE LINCOLN
COUNTY HISTORICAL ASSOCIATION.

of horses. There was a spring halfway up the island, and there was a cow flop beside it. One fellow wouldn't drink outa that spring, and he drank salt water instead. He had convulsions, and they had to tie him down. You can't drink salt water.

Margaret Libby

In 1918, my father bought a general store in Sandy Point. He and Mother and my sister took the horse and buggy up to Bucksport, crossed over on the ferry to Prospect, and went down to Sandy Point. The road from the ferry was pretty rough in April, running over ledges and frozen ground. They set up business in the store in Sandy Point—the building is still standing, though the rest are gone. I was born in November of that year.

We got around with a horse and buggy. My father took orders and delivered with a horse and wagon. In the winter, he had a pung with runners on it and used the horse to power the thing. That's how we got around until 1923, when he got his first car. It was a Star. He had to go to Portland to get it. He didn't know how to drive, but he got behind the wheel, and he drove home. Mother saw that vehicle out there and thought it was the most gorgeous thing she ever saw. Of course it was the ugliest thing you ever saw, really. After that, we traveled by car, but he delivered groceries with the horse until 1926 or 1927. We had the horse a long time after—my father couldn't bear to part with him. Pearl, his name was. It wasn't an uncommon male name back then. He was just out to pasture; we didn't do anything with him anymore.

It was an interesting store—he had everything you could think of, except the kitchen sink. He had thread and cloth and rubber boots and molasses in a barrel and vinegar in a barrel and flour and sugar in barrels. He had a candy cabinet and ice cream and sides of beef. After he got the car, my father would go to Bangor to pick things up. Before that, it came in on the train, and some of the local farmers would provide meat and so on.

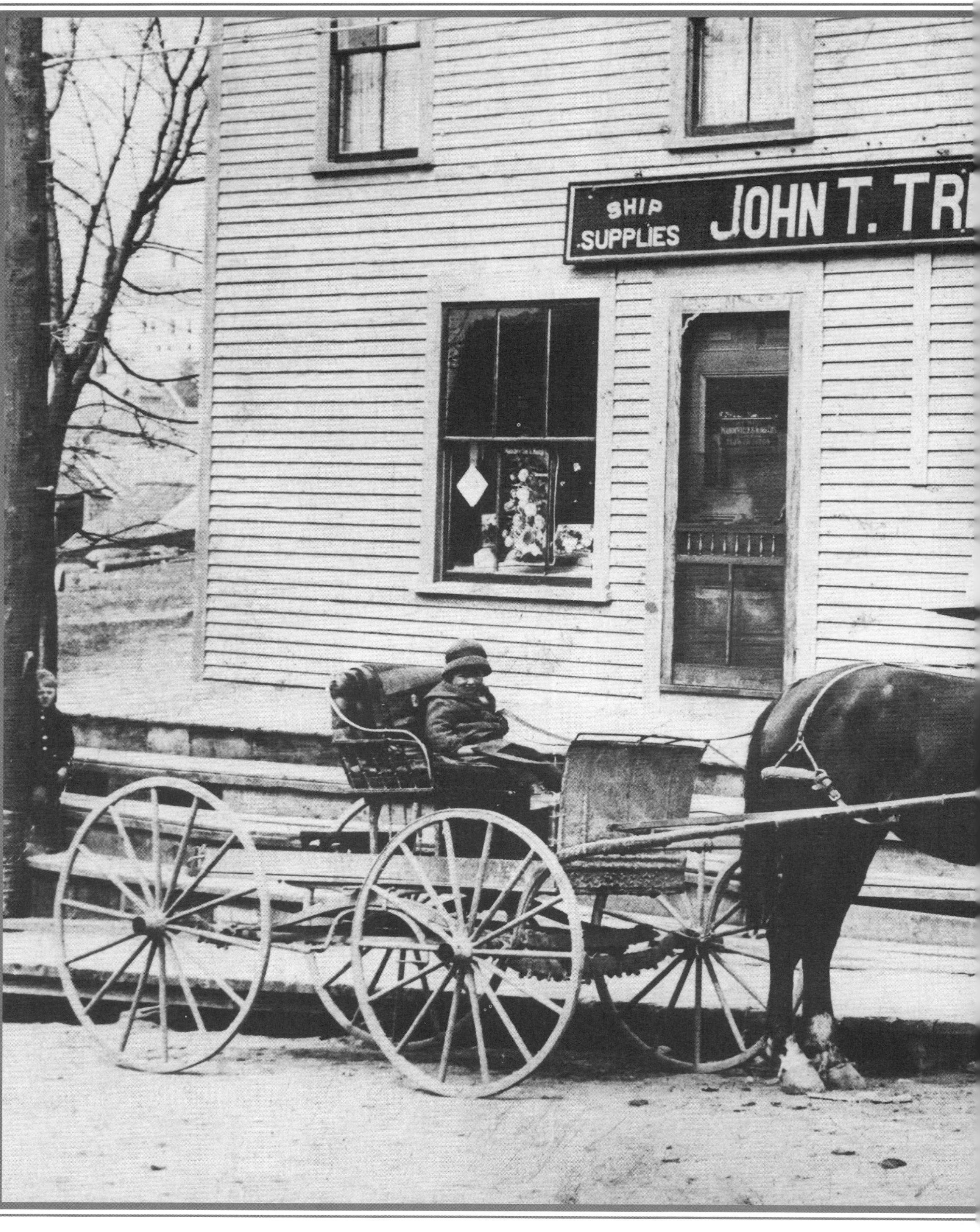
SHIP
SUPPLIES
JOHN T. TR

Stopping by the grocery store, Rockland, 1932.
FRANK CLAES COLLECTION.

Father would get a carload of grain from Bangor, and on weekends he'd get some young men to help him unload the car. Father would let me drive the pung from the store to the station. The horse was a big, powerful creature, and he liked to run. If he heard a train coming he'd go wild. I remember one time there were a couple of fellows standing on the back runners when he heard the train whistle and took off. Just as soon as he started running, they went off. I was hanging on for dear life, but we survived. He was frightened of trains and cars, but he was an awful good horse, really.

Once we were out taking orders around, and I was sitting on the seat next to my father. I had my hands in my pockets 'cause it was cold, and I was trying to keep them warm. It had rained recently, and we came down out of a driveway and there was a great ditch there. When the wagon hit the ditch, I pitched right forward under the horse's feet. Pearl seemed to know I was there, and he avoided me.

Frank Winchenbach
ROCKLAND · 1910s

There were one- and two-horse freight wagons that went to the Boston boat and the Maine Central Railroad. Now big trucks do ten or twenty times what they could. When Swift and Company changed from horses to automobiles, one feller drove down onto Tillson Avenue hollering, "Whoa! Whoa!"

Rena Bunker
MATINICUS · 1930s

In my day on Matinicus, they had horses. The storekeeper had a horse he used to deliver groceries with. A great big horse named Danny. I don't know what it was, but it was huge. The storekeeper died, and his wife had the horse and the farm or what was left of it. She was postmistress. She used to have a well down in the field, and she'd let Danny out of the barn to get a drink. She'd let him stay out and wander around, and then she'd go out and call him. He'd always come back to her and go into the barn. Well, one day she was sick. Her nephew Clayton lived next door, so she asked him to let Danny out for his water. "Won't he run off?" Clayton asked.

"Oh, no, he won't," she said, so Clayton let Danny out and he went down to get his drink. After a while, she said, "You better bring him back now. You just go out and call him."

That's just what he did, but Danny didn't pay any attention to Clayton at all. He called him three times, and the fourth time he hollered, "You son of a b__, you come here!" but Danny didn't come. Clayton went back to tell his aunt he couldn't get the horse in.

She'd heard the last call. "He's not used to being sworn at," she said. She went to call him herself, and Danny came right in.

Wasn't Clayton disgusted! "Well, he wouldn't come for me," he said.

"I wouldn't either," she said.

Bill Abbott
VERONA ISLAND • 1920s

My father had a horse. I don't remember his ever having a wagon, but the roads weren't plowed very good. He had a sleigh, but I only remember taking it out once or twice. He kept it up in the attic in the shed, hauled up on ropes. He also had a big double-runner sled, a pung, that had a set of runners in front about five feet across and another set behind. The back of the front runners were connected to the front of the back runners with crossed chains.

On top of each set of sled runners there was a bunker with post holes in each end. Posts were set in these holes when they'd haul long sections of trees out of the woods to be sawed up for firewood. Coming out of the woods with a load of firewood, as kids, we'd jump on the rear runner and have a free ride. If it was uphill, Father would make us get off and walk—the least load possible for the horse. When Father had to go to town for supplies, he would use just the front runners. He'd put a couple of planks across them to sit on and put on one for his feet. He'd hitch up old Fred, our horse, and bundle up in his big robe and head off for Bucksport. He claimed this was easier and warmer than fooling around with the sleigh.

Pair of horses with double-runner sled.
COURTESY OF THE LINCOLN COUNTY HISTORICAL ASSOCIATION.

Helen Reynolds
BROOKS • 1920s

The neighbor asked to borrow the horse, but he didn't say for what. Turned out he had to transport his dead uncle to the underpass and put him on the railroad. There was no way to do it but set him on the wagon seat and put an arm around him. It was an unusual, but very dignified, way to move a body.

Frank Winchenbach
1910s

There was a Finnish man who had a farm over in Warren. He had one of those big milk cans, the top of it held a quart, and he'd fill your bottle from that. He left in the morning and made his rounds, and his horse would go along and stop by himself at every house he was supposed to.

Roy Monroe
MILO · 1910s

There was a narrow bridge over the dam in town, not wide enough for two vehicles to pass, and occasionally someone would get nerved up and try to turn a six-horse hitch in the middle of the bridge. They could maneuver those horses something wonderful. Even when it was going on, it didn't seem possible. One pair of horses would be going by the sled at the same time that two pair were going ahead. It looked like a group of people countermarching.

I can remember when roads were rolled with a long-planked roller—the snow was just compressed. Grandfather moved two houses—one's out back here today. One good workhorse could pick up the weight of a story-and-a-half house and drag it over the snow.

Frank Winchenbach,
1920s AND 1930s

They used horses to haul the rock out of the quarries. They had two-horse teams, but those loads were heavy, and it was quite a slope coming up out of the quarry, so they'd hitch six horses on to come out of there. They used to whip the horses, but there was this one fellow who used to say, "Don't you touch that whip!" and he'd just cluck and away they'd go.

Leland Sherman
SEVEN HUNDRED ACRE ISLAND · 1930s

There was a workhorse, a big one, just one on the island. Everybody used to borrow him. He was the Gibsons' horse—his name was Pearly, I think. Sometimes he was balky. He was a funny devil—he could balk on nothin'. He'd look at it maybe and say "I ain't gonna pull that," but he could pull it if he'd a mind to. They didn't use him that much—that's why he was balky, I imagine, because they didn't use him much.

Forest Bunker
FRANKLIN

There were a lot of horses still, when I was a kid, but it changed fast. Up on the farm, they had three pair of horses doing the work, and the next thing you knew they had two tractors doing it all. That was in the early thirties.

In Bangor all those coal companies had horses. Everyone burned coal. There was black smoke everywhere. Today the environmentalists would all die of heart attacks. A lot of people didn't burn hard coal, they burned soft, because it was cheaper. That smoke was really black. They had a big barn down on Dutton Street, and every night there'd be a big parade going down to the barn. They had a guy, a hostler, all he done was look after those horses.

The fire vehicles was all pulled by horses, all but the main station and State Street—they had trucks. I saw it myself, how those horses stood in their stalls, and the alarm would ring. The same alarm rang in all the stations, and when that alarm came in, if it was for that station, a guy pulled a rope and that took the locks off the doors, and the doors flew open, and the horses came out and stood under the harnesses. They'd lower them down and do up a couple of snaps, and they were ready to go. Those horses knew exactly what they were going to do. The driver would sit up on his seat and pull another rope, and the big doors would open and he was on his way.

We used to jump on the rear sometimes if we could get on. Ted Morrison, that was his name, was good to us kids. He was an damn nice guy.

Frank Winchenbach
ROCKLAND · 1900s AND 1910s

Sure, I remember when there were fire horses. My wife's uncle had a horse that had been a fire horse, and very shortly after he got him, the alarm went off, and that horse ran to Station Number Four and began to back in. That's what they

Biddeford Fire Engines, 1908: The Eben Simpson, purchased in 1869 and named for the fire chief, and the first steam engine.

FROM THE MAINE HISTORICAL PHOTOGRAPH COLLECTION.

used to do, back in and they'd drop the harnesses right down onto them, and they'd be off.

Captain Bill Abbott
1920s

I remember going with my father to the blacksmith, Mr. Havener, in Bucksport. He'd have the bellows going, blowing on the fire. He'd get it hot enough and then he'd shove the shoe in there, and pull it out all red hot and pound on it, and drop it in the water. He'd do that again and again—sparks would fly. He had a leather apron on. He'd pick the horse's foot up and pound the nails into the poor old horse's hoof. It was really interesting.

Abbott Pattison
LINCOLNVILLE • 1920S

My sister and I rode our ponies down to Camden on US One twice a summer to be shod. There was a wonderful blacksmith down there on what's now Tannery Lane. Mr. Kirk, his name was. He was a little bent-over man. He used to get great big old draft horses to shoe, and supported them and their legs, fitting shoes. He had a big, heavy man who worked in the shop with him, who reminded me of Popeye's nemesis—a black-haired fellow. Mr. Kirk had the palest white skin, but was always soot-covered from the forge. Every Sunday he took the collection at the Episcopal Church in Camden, and he was always immaculate. His skin was as white as a sheet, and he always wore the same black or dark-blue suit.

Tom Flagg
LINCOLNVILLE • 1920S

I'd walk or hitchhike down to Kirk's blacksmith shop in Camden. He was an old man, doubled right over, and he always called me Boy. "Boy, you do this. Boy, you do that." There were two blacksmiths in that shop—Kirk and the big one with dark hair, Jones.

I'd watch and ask questions, and then Ed Goodwin—he was from out toward Hope—took me around with him and showed me what to do. I did all the work, and he looked on. When I got into high school I built my own shop. The shingles have all blown thin on it now, so you can tell how long ago that was. My uncle had a pair of mules—a horse couldn't stand it to go to Belfast and back every day, twenty-five miles, whereas a mule could take it, that's why he had mules. We put caulks on the shoes, and you had to sharpen them for ice. They

A blacksmith's shop.
FROM THE MAINE HISTORICAL PHOTOGRAPH COLLECTION.

had to sharpen the mules' caulks every day when it was icy—otherwise they'd slip and fall down and break their legs, or anyway not be able to go. We'd take the shoes off, sharpen the caulks, and put the shoes back on using the same nail holes. They finally come out with caulks you could drive in and screw in.

I shod horses for the rural route carriers, three of them, but that was about the last of the horses, other than workhorses. It's hard work to shoe them old big horses, I can tell you.

I made all kinds of other stuff. I made bridle chains to put on the runners when they were logging. Everybody owned a lot on the mountain. Everybody burnt wood—well, the rich people burnt coal, but most everybody burnt wood. It's some steep out there, and the horses couldn't hold the load back—you get a pair of horses with a cord or a cord and a half of wood on, it's heavy. So I made bridle chains for them. You'd stop the team, hook the chain around where the runner turns up in front, and hook the other end of the chain to the front bunk—that's part of the body. Then when you went ahead, it'd catch and grab. It'd fetch up when it got about in the middle of the runner. Then when you got to the bottom, you'd have to take the chain off, and it was bowstring tight, so I made these hooks that you'd hit a ring with your ax, and it'd slide off and you could unhook it.

Workhorses pulling a scoot.
COURTESY OF THE LINCOLN COUNTY HISTORICAL ASSOCIATION.

You had to make chain links one to a time, then, but people had plenty of time then.

I shod oxen a few times, but oxen were pretty much before my time. You had to hook them in a sling to shoe them—they wouldn't lift their foot up like a horse. You drove them into a frame thing and lifted them up and tied their foot up.

I had a yoke myself one time, a pair of steers. I had a wagon, but I don't know as I ever got them so they'd work much. I never much cared for oxen—they're too slow. Then cars came. A horse you can get on the side of the road, but oxen you couldn't get out of the way.

Peg Miller
LINCOLNVILLE • *1920s AND 1930s*

The men used to have a hay rack. They'd put in loose hay; no one ever heard of baled hay, in those days. A lot of barns burned. They did all the work with horses. My dad never had a tractor until I was in high school, but I learned to drive a car when I was eight or nine. I had three brothers, seven years between each of them, and I was the only girl, so I was spoiled rotten. I was the only granddaughter on one side, and on the other there were three, but I was the youngest, so I was spoiled.

I could drive the horses from tumble to tumble. They'd pile the hay in a tumble and then pick it up with the wagon, and different ones of us used to ride on top of the load treading. I hated to tread. I don't know why my dad had me do it—I was just a little bit of a thing.

Dad had a horse that was kind of fractious. They used to bring in a load of hay with the pair of horses, and then they'd unhitch one horse and bring him forward and tie him onto a rope through a pulley, and then they'd pick the hay all up with a big fork thing. You'd lead the horse forward, and it would raise the hay up into the hayloft. I was afraid of that horse, leading him out by the bridle, and didn't I hate to do it, so they decided to teach me to drive the car and put the rope onto the car. I knew reverse and low gear, and there were ruts you followed. I knew the place you stopped. If you didn't, that fork would take the roof off the barn. The car worked good.

Loading hay into a horse-drawn hay rack, Kezar Falls, 1938.

FROM THE GEORGE FRENCH COLLECTION, MAINE STATE ARCHIVES.

Working on the Narrow Gauge

Francis Haley

Francis Haley.
PHOTO BY
VIRGINIA L. THORNDIKE.

I was born in Madrid—that's Maˊ-drid, not like in Spain. In 1910, when I was born, and quite a while before that, the town was there. The house I was born in is missing now. Everybody I knew in the world once was in Phillips or Madrid, and now there's no one left. Well, people still live there, but I don't know any of them.

When I first moved into Portland, people wouldn't believe my snow stories, but then in 1952 or 1954 we had that awful snowstorm, and the snow drifted right up to the wires. That's how it was in Franklin County when I was growing up. One winter, our neighbor, Frank Harnden, died at home, and the roads weren't open. He had two grown boys living at home, eighteen or twenty, and they took the toboggan and went on snowshoes and took the body to the undertaker in Phillips. I was young, and dead people were something strange to me, gave me the shivers, but they had to do it.

My family had horses—my grandfather, and my father did, but I never owned a horse in my life. I still love them.

Father told about a colt he'd bought from my grandfather, who raised him. Father used the colt in the buggy when he was only two or three years old. One day, he drove the buggy up to Charlie Smith's store. Charlie Smith had been a brakeman on the train, and some kind of an accident had left him with a stiff leg—he used to have one crutch. He opened up a general store in Madrid. The Sandy River went through there, and the road went alongside the river, the way they do. It was in a valley—the sides rose up steep some places. Charlie's place, because of the bank, was up above the road. You went up half a flight of stairs to go into the store.

So, my father drove up, threw the reins down, and went into the store to get a plug of tobacco or something. There was a fellow there told him not to leave that colt alone, he'd go home. My father said, "You couldn't even send him home."

The fellow gave the colt a slap on the rump, and off he went. My father came out of the store and hollered to him, and the colt turned the buggy right around and came back. Then to show off, my father backed up the stairs, and the colt came up the stairs, too. They had to unharness him to turn him around.

My father never owned a car. He always had a good horse—never got out of the horse-and-buggy days. He'd always had a team, and a good one. Then cars started to come in, and I can remember his disgust. A fellow wanted to buy one of his horses, and he sold him. "I got sick of riding in the gutter anyway," he said. When you saw a car coming, you'd turn out because you wouldn't want him to get stuck or something.

My father was a foreman for the Sandy River two-foot railroad—went into Madrid Junction and then five or six miles out to the lumber camp Number Six. At the museum in Portland now they've got some of the same cars that were on that railroad when I was a kid.

He had one horse, a mare, that knew the railroad trip about as well as he did. When a big snowstorm came, the switches would freeze or get ice built up in them, and they'd have a lot of wrecks, so they'd have to go out and clean the switches before they plowed the tracks. They had to hand-clean them, and he'd take the sleigh out. The road crossed the tracks a lot, and she knew the area so well he could drive to the first crossing and then tie the reins up and let the horse go on while he waded through to clean the switches. She'd have a place she'd go—say, Curtis Lawrence's farm—and she'd wait for him there. Now, I don't want to make her seem too smart—she'd been there before, when he might have stopped there for his lunch and put her in the barn and fed her—but it was pretty good, just the same.

Then finally one day, an engineer told him she had come down to a crossing, and she'd come real near the tracks and paced as fast as she could, then she broke into a gallop. For some reason, she thought she had to beat the train to the crossing. Fortunately, they had enough time to stop the train, but my father never could let her go alone again.

One of my favorite dogs got killed by a train—a little black spaniel, she was. My father would sometimes take her to work with him. One day the crew was working across the Sandy River, and she left home and decided to join them. She got on the bridge, and she was hit and killed. The engineer felt terrible—all those men knew her and played with her.

That bridge is gone now—quite a big bridge it was, too.

When I was a baby and very small, Dad had a white mare he called Babe. She was a Wilkes-strain horse. They were supposed to be kind of spicy, hard to take care of, but tough and fast. She'd never been raced, but he used her as a buggy horse, and he'd brag about goin' to visit his uncle in Lancaster, New Hampshire, a hundred and twenty-five miles away. He'd feed her at three or four in the morning and start out, and he'd drive till it got hot around eleven. Then he'd stop and turn her out in somebody's pasture, pull the harness off, and turn her loose for a couple of hours, and then start up again. He'd drive till late at night, and maybe take a little rest in the middle of the night, and he'd be in by noon the next day. They used to say that was either a hell of a trip or a lie.

I can't remember her, but I think I know just what she looked like.

He got her when she was only a three year old. A pair of girls had bought her, school teachers, and she wasn't very well broke. It was when automobiles were just coming in, and every time she'd see one, she'd smash up the wagon and

Bridgton and Harrison Railway railbus at Bridgton station, 1938.
COURTESY OF
ROBERT MACDONALD.

go home. She hurt the girls a couple of times, and they wanted to get rid of her, so he traded an older mare to them for her. He knew she had to get used to cars, so he'd take his whip and check her up high and go to town. Then, when she saw a car and acted up, he'd give her quite a licking. She'd been in the habit of breaking the buggy and heading home, but he got her so my mother used to drive her.

When I was older, I had a horse to use, two winters. It was an old horse named Pomp, fifteen years old, that had a lot of miles on him, hard work. Some doctor used to own him. I used to take him to school in the winter with the sleigh. I'd take my brother and sister and pick up the two Harnden kids along the way, Delma and Zelda. Aren't those interesting names? We lived a mile and a half from school, and when we got there, I'd tie up the reins so they wouldn't drag, and Pomp would go home and my mother would put him away. The mailman used to meet him halfway home, and he said, "He's pretty good. He'll turn out a little bit, but he won't give me the whole road." We'd walk home from school. Pomp never did learn to come back for us.

I never will be very good with an automobile. I was brought up with horses. My father did drive an old Model T for a year, but it belonged to the railroad. They bought this car and told my father he had to drive it—I don't know how happy he was about that. They decided it would be easier for him to drive the crew up to a crossing near where they were going to work, instead of fooling around with a handcar.

He ran Number Six—they had sections of track that were five or six miles long, and the crew was responsible for "keeping it up," as they called it. The track went up to Rangeley, and at Madrid Junction, where we lived, a line went off to the side—that was Number Six. They'd have to go over every bit of it each year.

A narrow-gauge construction crew at Head Tide cut, ca. World War I.
COURTESY OF LINCOLN COUNTY HISTORICAL ASSOCIATION.

They'd look for spreads, as they called them—after trains ran over the track long enough, the spikes would wiggle and come out or get loose, and the rails spread.

They had a gauge they carried with them to measure the distance, but their eye got good, too. They'd get on a handcar going home and every so often, they'd say, "I think there's a spread there," and they'd stop and fix it. If the spike was loose, they had a thing that had an end on it like a cow's hoof, and they'd jam that thing under the spike and pull it. They had plugs about six inches long, made of wood, three-quarters of an inch square, and they'd drive those into the holes the spikes came out of to tighten it up. If they had to move the track, they had long bars, and two or three men would line up in a row and jab the point of their bars in the dirt, and the foreman would call out, "Now, now, now!" and they'd work together to get the rail moved back where it belonged.

On a curve, the outside rail had to be higher, and they'd have to run that in from level to steep in the center of the curve to level again when it straightened back out. If the track wasn't right, you'd notice, 'specially if you were riding in the engine—it would lurch you around. If it was the way it should be, even if the train was going full speed, the passengers would never know there was a curve.

They had levels with notches in them, a quarter of an inch each time. On a big curve, the rail would probably be an inch higher on the outside. They'd set the level across the tracks and put the notch on the rail and pull it back, and then they'd go on a little farther and set it another notch and another notch and then back again. It took a lot of brain to figure it out, but a lot of the workers could do that work even though they never went to school.

There were some real characters working up there. There was a fellow, John Wyman, who weighed 280 or 300 pounds and was so strong. And in the same crew was Vance Whitney, a little bit of a man with a huge mustache. He was very comical—people used to almost work for nothing to work with him. There was a show going all day long. John Wyman was known for having the best section, smooth as could be.

Then there was Dinky Leavitt. His name was Fred, actually, but they called him Dinky because he was so small. He was an engineer, a good engineer in the summer, but he wasn't good at plowing snow. On those engines there was a big lever to switch from forward to reverse. Plowing snow, you'd get stuck in a big drift. You'd surge forward until you'd spin the wheels and couldn't go, and then you'd throw that big lever to reverse. It was all manual, and took a lot of power. Dinky Leavitt was not good at plowing snow, but it only happened a couple of times each winter, and he was a good engineer.

It was hard work, hot work, mostly shoveling gravel. Every summer they had to completely surface the railway. They had to grass it—pull out all the grass and weeds and tamp it all down. They did so much a day. Even down on the broad gauge they have to do that still, but they have a special car. It's all done mechanically, now.

The sections were usually five miles, and there was a foreman and two or three helpers. We lived at Madrid Junction, and one helper lived there, too. Carroll Plummer lived in Madrid Village. He was a big, heavy man, red-faced and always laughing. He had a handcar—a miserable thing. It was one of those you pump up and down. On the downgrade you didn't have to pump much, but that thing would pump up and down on its own, and you had to be watching not to get hit on the head with those darn things. It was all downgrade on the way out, but a hard return home. Then they got a crank car—that was an improvement.

They had those cars they built from automobiles, built by fellows who worked on the railroad. Orris Vose was general manager. They built him a car—a REO, I think it was. They put railroad wheels underneath it. You'd just get on that thing and go. They had a train-bus kind of thing, too, built out of a truck. (It's a funny name, Orris, and he had a brother, an engineer up in Kingfield, whose name was Flave. Flave was a nice-looking man—the women always used to chase him. He was tall and had broad shoulders.)

It's hard to get a steam engine ready—it takes hours to get it going and build up the steam. Those old engines all ran on soft coal. I had a job on the transfer crew in the summers when I was in high school. In Farmington, where the broad gauge came in, they had sidings where they could back a car in next to the narrow gauge, and the transfer crew worked there. The worst thing we had to transfer was coal. It was all hand done. Down in the city, they had ramps built up, and they'd open a sliding hatch and send the coal down a chute to where they wanted it to go, but we had to do it all by hand. It was a hot job. It wasn't that bad once you got to the bottom if the steel was smooth—then you could get your shovel underneath—but up on top or in the middle, particularly with a square-across shovel, you had to keep wiggling it around and get some coal on and throw it over. Then they got some special shovels, halfway between a shovel and a spade, and that was better, but it was still awful work. Of course they needed a lot of coal. Not only did the engines run on it, but the passenger cars all had coal stoves in them for heat. We had grain and everything to transfer over, too.

I also went to a little shed by the track to dry sand. That was a little railroad job that most people don't know about. They'd screen the sand so all the rocks were out of it, but it would still be damp and would stick together. It had to be dry so it would run. They had a little stove with a tin funnel-shaped thing on the outside of it that held a couple of bushels. I'd get a good fire going, with soft coal, and then shovel sand from the heap up into this thing around the stove. It was dusty work, and the stinking coal smoke was real miserable. They'd place a container on the engine and keep that full of dry sand so when the track got wet or icy and the wheels started spinning, they'd pull a rope and the sand would run down on the track.

The most ashamed I ever was, was when I was a teenager and was working on the spare crew, resurfacing a piece of track between Kingfield and Carrabasset. They were using flat cars to shovel gravel on. Up there, they could

A Wiscasset, Waterville, and Farmington Railroad engine and crew.
COURTESY OF THE LINCOLN COUNTY HISTORICAL ASSOCIATION.

drive the train up, but there was no place to turn around, and they had to back the train into Strong village. Harl White was on that train, and when it got time to leave I got on the flat car with him. We came around a sharp corner, going backward, and I was looking at the track and thought the needles were the wrong way, that the switch was wrong. I hollered to Harl, "The switch is off!"

When they hook the cars together, they have the coupler, but they also have a rubber hose with a brake lever on it. Harl put the brakes on, and then I saw the switch was right. Jeez, that was a terrible thing! But Harl said it was better to be safe than to run off the rails. I was embarrassed, but he never criticized me for it.

I never saw such a hard-working fellow as Harl White. When he had a crew out there working, he had to go back a ways to sight down the track and see when it was right, and he'd run like a son of a gun. He always had his own shovel, too. He didn't have to, he was the foreman, but he'd work right along with them. He had a brother Perley—can you imagine that name, Perley White?—and he was a real hellion, liked to drink and play and have fun rather than work.

In 1935 the railroad went bankrupt, and they cut up all those engines and sold them for iron. Iron happened to be high then. They sold the rails, too. There were two fellows that were given a job up the Rangeley area yarding up the rails as they were taken out. They had these two teams of horses, bought at auction in Farmington and trucked up to these two men to yard out the rails. There used to be a horse dealer in Farmington who brought horses in from the West. Most of them were pretty raw when they came in. These two teams looked beautiful, they'd be good in the show ring—a gray team and a bay team, maybe they were.

A load for those horses would be one row of rails on the beams, not stacked up, and they'd have to sack up the hills anyway. Goodness, where'd that come from? I haven't used that expression in years. Sacking a load, that's when the horses are digging, bent right down. They just walk when the going's good.

Both those men were old-time horsemen, and after the first day's work they were talking. "By God, my off horse wants to trot all the time, and the near one's lazy," said one of them.

"Well, why don't we switch them tomorrow, two quick ones and two lazy ones?" said the other man. And they did that, and they both had pretty good teams then, even if they didn't look so good. One fast team, one slow. It's a funny thing—you put two lazy ones together, they both have to work.

A converted truck and automobile transport an inspection team on the Sandy River narrow gauge tracks, 1933.

COURTESY OF ROBERT MACDONALD.

Trains

Forest Bunker
FRANKLIN

When I was a kid, it took a long time to go anywhere. People didn't travel much—they stayed home. If they went, they'd probably go on the train, if they could, for the comfort. Even as a kid, railroading was what I always wanted to do. And today, if a train goes by, I stop and look at it.

The Canadian National and the Canadian Pacific ran right in front of the house in New Brunswick where I was when I was a kid. I never missed a train. I was always crazy about them. First time I rode on one was in 1918, when I went from Bangor to Van Buren. My mother came from New Brunswick, and we went up there to the farm for the summer. I spent all my summers there till I got too big and had to go to work. They used to put us on the train, my sister and me. The train would leave at 3:30 in the morning, and they'd take us down to the station and get us a ticket. The old conductor, Mike Haggerty—I'll remember his name for the rest of my life—he would see we got to Van Buren, and he'd see we kept in line on the way. We got there about 11 o'clock in the morning. The train stopped at every damn town you came to, almost.

My first love was the railroad. They did everything by hand then. On the Bangor and Aroostook, they had to tamp the whole track every year, and they had a steel gang must have had two hundred men on it. They'd lift the track, a whole line of them with their shovels, tamp, lay steel. They only had a short time—they started in May and shut it down in October. Then, of course, the guys would all quit and go picking potatoes.

I worked for the Bangor and Aroostook from 1942 until 1975. No matter how hard it was, I never griped about it. You go to bed with the old lady and everything is cozy, and then the phone rings at one or two in the morning: "I gotta have you for a plow train." You gotta get up and go. But I loved it, and I wouldn't want to do anything else.

Standard Gauge

The Sandy River and Rangeley Lakes Railroad narrow gauge meets the Maine Central train from Portland at Farmington, 1920.

COURTESY OF
ROBERT MACDONALD.

My first job for them was fireman on a steam engine. It was a hard job—you had to take what no one else wants, it's all done on seniority, and you get the bones. But then I got called into the army and when I got back two years later, I had gained ten years' seniority, enough people had left so I got way ahead. It's interesting work, dirty work. I'd do it again if they ever came back. It was quite a challenge, running the steam engine. You had to be the boss. If you weren't, it was just as contrary as anything you ever saw. One fellow said it was just like a woman—you never knew what the hell it'd do next. There were twelve engines at the B&A, all supposed to be just alike, but they were all different—you had to learn how to get the power out of every one of them.

Contrary to what everyone thinks, on those steam engines it was very cold in the winter, cold and drafty. The cab was just set on the end of that boiler, and every place they wanted to put a pipe out through it, they drilled a hole three times big enough for the pipe. When you were running a snowplow, you couldn't see across the cab, the snow was flying so. Your feet would get so cold you could hardly walk on them—you sat there like a dummy and froze.

There's a lot happens on a train people never know about. The conductor, he feels pretty good back there in the passenger cars, but who brings you home safely is the engineer and the fireman, though they never get credit for it. If anything ever goes wrong, you derail or anything, the first question always is, "How fast were you going?" If you were going under the speed limit, then they had to find someone else to blame. The guy who took care of the track, he says, "Well, there's nothing wrong with my track, my track's perfect." Whenever an engineer got killed in an accident, a collision with another train or something, they always found a way to blame him. He couldn't say otherwise.

The big business of the B&A was pulp, paper, and potatoes. The three Ps. Great Northern Paper Company was the biggest customer. They got seventy-five to one hundred cars a day in the summertime, wood that had been cut the winter before and stockpiled near the railroad. When they were shipping potatoes in winter, they had four hundred and fifty to five hundred cars a day, twenty-two tons to the car. Just think of it—you had to bag them things and then load them all onto cars—and every damn bit of it was done by hand then.

I worked for thirty-three years for the railroad and drove thirty miles to work every day. I was only late once, and I could have stayed at home that day, because after I got there, there was nothing moving for four or five hours. That was after a big snowstorm.

I've known people who'll exaggerate a little to make a better story, or stretch it. An old conductor I once knew told this story and said it was true; I can't say it isn't, but I don't know as it is. They were coming down one night and the brakes set, emergency. They locked up—the train had parted into two pieces. They put it back together again and hooked up the air on it and kept on going. The next day they found a lumber car down the bank. They claimed it had jumped out from between those other cars. Well, it's possible, but I'd like to have seen it.

Anything I told you is the truth. I'm not a bunkhouse lawyer—those are the guys who stood up and told stories.

Pete Ascher
1930s AND 1940s

We lived in New Harbor and used to go up to Newcastle on the train to meet different ones in the family. The west-bound trains used to take water there, and if the passenger train was late, I'd get to watch the freight trains. There was a fellow, Ike Stowell, who could actually run up and down the side ladders of freight trains. It intrigued me—how could he do it? He was a human fly. I was ten or eleven years old then, and I worked with him, years later.

One time I was holding down the baggage car on the Bar Harbor Express, going from Rockland to Portland. We had steam engine Number 470, the last on the Maine Central, run by a hot-shot engineer, Broadway Pete.

I made a point to inspect the rolling stock for which I was responsible, and this time I discovered a hobo standing up in the doorway of the baggage car, behind the tender. Well, he might not have been a hobo, he might have been a Knight of the Road. What's a Knight of the Road? Well, that's a hobo. There were two ways hobos rode, "riding the rods," under a freight car, and "riding the blind." That's what he was doing. That was perhaps the most meager of accommodations on our posh train of some ten Pullmans.

Well, along about that time, a well-dressed woman came up with a little poodle. She handed me a bowl of dog food, a five-spot, and Fi-Fi. "Here, you take care of Fi-Fi," she said, "and I'll see you in Philadelphia." She didn't wait for me to tell her I was only going to Portland, she was gone.

By this time, the man on the blind was consuming proportionately as much belched-up cinders as the Number 470 was in fuel. It was time to open the end door and see if he wanted to be rescued. "Come on in here," I called.

He gratefully stumbled inside the baggage car and shook off some of his cinders.

"Where do you think you're going?" I asked him.

Maine Central Railroad's Bar Harbor Express, Northern Maine Junction, 1938. This premium train provided service to New York and Philadelphia, with a steamboat connection at Bar Harbor in the summer.
COURTESY OF ROBERT MACDONALD.

"Portland," he said.

"Do you accept the concept of Brotherly Love?"

"Oh, yes," he cheerfully responded.

"Then you're going to Philadelphia, the City of Brotherly Love. You take care of Fi-Fi, and maybe a lady there will give you five dollars," I said. After all, a fin was a half-run's pay, back in those days.

I never heard anything about it, so I guess it turned out OK.

We had a guy on the Mountain Division named Gigiere, a flagman. The run went from Portland to St. Johnsbury; it'd stop in Sebago Lake to take water, then go puffing along awhile. This one night, along about Raymond, Maine, the train went emergency. It was stopped, and I went out to inspect everything, but I couldn't find anything wrong. I think everybody but me knew what it was. Well, we got up to St. Johnsbury about noon. It was a long run, fourteen hours, and I went back to the caboose to clean up. There's Gigiere with a big chef's hat on, and he's singing, happy as can be, and you could smell wonderful food. There's bushel baskets of vegetables and all sorts of things all over the caboose. "Come in, boy, and eat like a king," says Gigiere.

The next day, it was still a little bit daylight when we went by where we'd stopped the night before. "Look at that garden," they said to me. "Cleaned out, ain't it?"

Eddie Clark was flagman on the Number One, the local from Portland to Bangor. Sometimes I'd catch that off the extra board if there were extra cars on it. The Belfast branch used to come up to Burnham Junction and set across the wooden platform from Number One, and we'd get the milk cans and so on from it. There was a four hundred-pound fireman on the Belfast branch. He couldn't get in the cab except by climbing over the firebox. The fireman on the Number One was a very heavy man, too. One day, the fellow on the Belfast line waddled across the platform to the Number One and started to climb up to talk to his friend. Clark was standing back by the coach, but he could hear his engineer hollering, "Get down! Get down! Two of us on here'll tip this goddam engine over!"

Then there's another story. This conductor on the Pine Tree Limited—a nice old man, good as gold, and always good to me—was not what you'd call dapper. He was left over from the turn of the century. When the train crew got over to Bangor, they'd go over to the Adams—that was a flophouse across from the station. Everyone gathered there for beer and a meal, and you could sleep upstairs for fifty cents. The crewmen would go up there and sleep. Well, the story was—it's a fable, really—that the old conductor was asleep, and the brakeman got hold of his vest. They poured a kettle of hot water through it and come up with a bowl of soup.

They called me one day for the baggage car on the Number Ninety-three, the local passenger train from Bangor to Vanceboro. It was a two-car train, baggage and coach. Then we'd catch the Number Eight back; that was the big train of the division. On our local you did everything—you even stopped at flag stops and picked up hunters and fishermen. It was a rinky-dink train.

Well, this one day, on the manifest was a Railway Express shipment of ice cream, a couple of tubs, for Wytopitlock. I suppose the local store had run out of ice cream. We got to Wytopitlock, and I put all the stuff off—the mail, the baggage, and whatever else. We whistled off and proceeded. Halfway to the next station, I discovered I hadn't put the ice cream off. It was going to melt! I decided to take it over to Vanceboro, hoping there was enough dry ice there. Then I was going to put it on the Number Eight, and if I couldn't convince them to stop, I'd just roll it off as we went through. Well, the Number Eight used to go like a bat out of hell; they didn't waste any time. By the time I'd rolled that stuff off, at sixty miles per hour, it landed over around West Wytopitlock, in the woods.

I challenge any trainman on the Maine Central to state they haven't had a similar experience.

Willard Wilson
CUMBERLAND CENTER

My first ride on a train was in October 1936, when my father and I went to the Topsham Fair. We walked two and a half or three miles to the station. The train came through about 9 or 9:30, and we had to put the flag out to tell them to stop for us. We boarded the train and went to Brunswick. It was fun for me, being a seven year old. Then we walked from Brunswick to the fairgrounds, and the really wild thing, I remember today, was walking across the railroad bridge over the Androscoggin River, between Brunswick and Topsham. My father turned around to look at me, and there I was on my hands and knees. It was scary, looking down on the water, and I was afraid I'd fall off, so I went down on my hands and knees.

Lawrence Brown

I worked forty-three years for the Maine Central Railroad. Been everything, gandy dancer and all. A gandy dancer is the guy who packs the dirt down under the ties. I started out as a bus driver out of Bangor, on the run to Quebec City and Portland. Then they sold out to Greyhound, and I wouldn't work for Greyhound—their head was higher than ours. I got a job with the Maine Central as a carpenter. Let's see, I retired in 1975, so that was in 1932.

I lived in Dixmont as a kid, and my father used to haul pulpwood to Etna and load it on special train cars. He was a farmer, and he used to haul milk to Carmel, to the Turner Center Creamery. I used to go with him on weekends, with either two horses or four horses on the sled, depending on the going.

I got acquainted with these railroads before going to school. When I was a kid in grammar school, we lived behind the station in Newport, Maine. The train used to come in from Hartland. I got acquainted with the engineer and the fireman when they was layin' over, and I'd ride around the yard with them in the engine. I don't believe I was more than ten or twelve.

My brother and I used to ride on the train from Detroit to school in Newport. My father was working for the state that year, measurin' rocks for a rock crusher they were bringin' in to Detroit. The job was just one season, and we'd already started school over in Newport, so we'd take the train. The train we come home on in the afternoon was the Number Forty-eight out of Bangor, the milk train. The Number Forty-eight, they used to say, stopped at everybody's house,

A Maine Central milk train.

COURTESY OF THE LINCOLN COUNTY HISTORICAL ASSOCIATION.

and at a two-story house she stopped twice. It ran from Bangor to Portland, stopping at every station. Some places didn't have an agent—where we got on didn't. I had to put the flag up to flag the train down. Then when they stopped, the brakeman or the conductor would run out and take the flag down so it wouldn't bother anyone. After I got used to it, I'd take the flag down again to save them gettin' off. It was a green flag on a stick two and a half or three feet long. You'd put it in the holder.

Then when I was runnin' bus from Rumford to Bethel, I'd go down and back in the morning, and again in the early evening, and in between, too. I got acquainted with the engineer and fireman in Bethel, and they used to let me run the engine from the roundhouse to the station when they went out in the afternoon. I was settin' on gold then.

I lived in Belgrade till we moved here a year ago. Out there, the railroad track was fifty feet from my garage. Now it's eight hundred feet from me. An engine came through at one o'clock this morning and gave me a salute whistle. I recognized it. When we first moved here, the neighbors asked why the trains whistle so much, and I told them, "New kid on the block."

I'm still railroading. I had a triple bypass, so I have to behave myself. Last Sunday I was down to Alna helping with the Narrow Gauge there. I can't do much work anymore, but I take stuff down that they can use. I've collected a lot of stuff over the years.

Rosella Loveitt
SOUTH PORTLAND · 1920S AND 1930S

I loved the train. It used to run up to Boston; there was an Eastern Division and a Western. One went by way of Portsmouth and the other through Dover. The Flying Yankee made a very fast trip from Boston to Bangor. When I was a student at the University of Maine I used to take the Flying Yankee home. I graduated in 1930.

My first teaching job was in Kezar Falls. It was during the Depression years, and positions were very hard to get. I boarded up there, and if I came home on the weekend, I'd go down to Cornish and take the Mountain Division train home. When the weather was good, my father would drive me, but in the winter he wouldn't have the car out so much, so I used to take the train.

I was a great sports fan. We used to go up to Boston at least once a year to see the Boston Red Sox and take the train back again. Later on, after I learned to drive, I'd take my father up in the car.

I miss the trains very much. It would be wonderful if they brought them back.

Captain Bill Abbott
1930s

I can just remember going on the train the first time, Bangor to Bucksport. I must have been about ten. That train left at eleven at night and didn't get in till seven or eight in the morning. It stopped every little place. At one place around Newport, they didn't actually stop, but they slowed down and threw off one Sunday newspaper.

Margaret Libby
STOCKTON SPRINGS · *1920s*

I used to ride the railroad to Prospect to take piano lessons. After the lesson, I'd walk back down to the station and flag the train. The flag was kept right outside the door, and you'd pick it up and wave it and hold your breath, hoping they'd stop. One time they didn't, and I had to walk home. It's an awful feeling to see that train going by.

Gerene Hunt
WYTOPITLOCK · *1920s*

I was on the school basketball team—we had boys' and girls' teams. Most of the other towns we went to for games, we went on the train. Usually we stayed overnight at people's houses, and then when they came to return the game they stayed with some of us. One night we played Lee. We went to Mattawamkeag by train, and then from there to Lee in cars. The railroad had orders to pick us up in Mattawamkeag about 11 o'clock. It was a Canadian Pacific train, and they claimed they didn't have the order—anyway, they didn't stop. So we were there till seven in the morning. We stayed in the station, where they kept a good fire going. The principal had to go to Bangor for some reason, so we were all alone there—a bunch of teenagers. The boys would get warm and take their jackets off, and we girls would appropriate them and put our heads on them for pillows. First thing we knew, the boys'd whisk them out from under us.

Oh, no, we weren't angry that the train didn't stop for us. It was fun, a big experience.

Phil Hatch
RANGELEY · 1920s

When I was a boy, we spent summers in the Rangeley area. The train ran from Portland to Rumford through Bemis—Bemis is no longer in existence—to Oquossoc. Those were the old coal steam trains, and I remember that if you opened a window because it was hot, you were black by the time you got there. The engines had to work hard to go over the mountains, and of course, kids my age were always dressed in white. We had these little Palm Beach suits, with neckties. My mother, too—she wore high-necked white dresses with big hats. We'd be absolutely black.

Richard Sexton
1910s

We always took the Bar Harbor Express to and from Philadelphia, and while it didn't impress me much at the time, it was the most comfortable and elegant means of travel I've ever known. Looking back on it, I see that it was much better than the flying cattle cars we have to travel on today.

To go home, we would get on the train in Rockland at five in the afternoon and then we'd sail happily into Portland. There they put on a diner, and we were attached to the main body of the Bar Harbor Express (there were five sections altogether, from Rangeley, Kineo, Bar Harbor, and some other place). Then off you went again. You had a delicious dinner, and you'd retire and sleep comfortably and wake up as you pulled out of Penn Station in New York. They had put a new diner on for breakfast, and you'd get to Philadelphia at 9:30 in the morning, having had a good night's sleep and two beautiful meals.

Going the other way, it all worked in reverse: they picked up the morning diner at Portland, and it rode with us all the way up to Rockland. When my brother and I had grown to where we were reasonably independent, we would get out at Portland. There were seven tracks, I think it was, all under cover. We'd take the number of our car with us and scamper off to do something in the station—watch the engines coming and going—and then we had to pick out which train our car was in and rejoin it.

The trains were most commodious and comfortable, and the Bar Harbor Express was the gilt-edged exhibit of them all. You never had a jiggle or a jig—it was absolutely out of this world. In the summer, there were three complete trains a day, round-trip. We all took it for granted, as we did all the things that we have no longer.

Traveling in those days was a great joy, a great pleasure. Today it's an awful feeling—the roar, sitting so close to a stranger. It's ghastly. I'm afraid I'll never see comfortable travel again. In those days, they had the principle of making travel comfortable so you'd go that way again. They made all sorts of accommodations for you. There was a porter who put you on the train and put your bag over your seat for you. It was all very civilized and nice.

It was harder in those days as far as speed goes, but speed isn't everything.

Richard Sexton
1920s

> The Train Ferry over the Kennebec

When you got to Bath on the train, there was no bridge; instead, there was a ferry, a great big ferry with three tracks on it. When the train came in, it was broken up into three sections and pushed onto the ferry. My brother and I used to get up and watch the train being broken up. The tracks led right down to the water, of course, to get to the ferry. They would load one third of the train on one side, and the thing sank way down. Then they'd load the next third on the other side and it would level out again. They'd load the rest of the train and the engine in the middle. When they got to the other side of the river, the engine took one section off, backed up and got another section, and backed up again for the last third. It all took time, and when we went home at the end of the summer, it was all done after dark.

In the very early days, the family sent a groom ahead by freight train, with two horses and the carriage, and he was there to meet us when we came in. It was quite a normal thing for people to do when they came for the summer in those days. We had a house in Camden then, and a nice barn there.

The groom made history in the family: Once when he was parked at Bath in the freight car waiting for the ferry, he felt the car begin to rumble. He knew there was no engine attached, and the car was headed for the water. Fortunately he was very athletic, so he shot up the outside and got hold of the brake and stopped the car. He saved our family's horses with his quick action.

We only had horses until I was three or four. I don't remember them, actually. I never liked horses an awful lot. The groom became the chauffeur, and he worked for the family for fifty-eight years.

The Maine Central railroad car ferry Hercules *crossing the Kennebec River between Bath and Woolwich, early 1900s.*

COURTESY OF ROBERT MACDONALD.

Parker Marean
WISCASSET

The regular train went to Rockland from Portland. When I was really young, we came up on that train a couple of times. It was an awful ordeal. The train had to come across the ferry at the Kennebec. They had to break up the train and load it on the ferry, and it took a long time. After they built the bridge, in the thirties, things got faster. Now they're getting just as slow again, with all the traffic.

Charlie Libby
1920s

When we lived in New York we came up summers and sometimes for Christmas. I remember one trip in particular. Usually when the train got to Bath, they'd put the cars on the ferry and bring them over to Woolwich. But this time, it was a Sunday, and the passengers got off the train, got on the ferry, and got on another set of cars at Woolwich. Well, there was a big black stove in the new car, and to me it looked as big as anything. I took one look at that stove, and I didn't stop howling till we got off at Rockland.

The Narrow Gauge Railroad

Parker Marean
WISCASSET · 1920s

I used to go all the way up to Albion on the narrow gauge a couple of times a summer. My father would take me up. He used to get off in China and fish in China Lake sometimes—there were a lot of fish there then. Sam Sewell was running the train then, and he used to take us out for a ride in that Model T they had rigged up with wheels for the rails.

Often we'd take the narrow gauge in the morning and only go as far as Head Tide—that's eight miles up the Sheepscot River. We'd take a picnic and stay all day. We'd go swimming. They used to have a rope, and you could swing out over the water. We were too young then to ride our bicycles up there. Someone older always went with us to make sure we didn't drown.

The narrow gauge was a regular deal then—I'd see it every day. The family owned a little island called Howe Island—it's where the sewage treatment plant is now. We used to swim down there when the tide was right. From half tide to high it was fine, but at low tide, it was nothing but mudflats. The narrow gauge was always busy running by, across to the town.

Frank Winchenbach
1920s and 1930s

The Rockport-Rockland Lime Company had four engines, and the tracks went around the city. They hauled lime rock down from the quarries and dumped it in the kilns, and they hauled coal from the barges. Quite often the coal would catch fire—soft coal does that, you know. We used to live right in front of the tracks—the wind blowin' just so would get your clothes out on the line all black.

The lime kilns used to pay forty cents an hour. They were all wood-fired. Ships used to haul the cordwood in. I worked there one time. I was small, so I could stand in the hold and pass that cordwood over, and anybody any bigger would have to duck. The first day, I worked like the devil and got all loaded up quick, and when I got my check they'd taken off an hour and a half. The next time, I went slower.

Rockport Railroad, serving the lime kilns.
FRANK CLAES COLLECTION.

The narrow gauge, Wiscasset.
COURTESY OF THE LINCOLN COUNTY HISTORICAL ASSOCIATION.

TRAINS 99

Trolleys

Albert Chatfield

We had a street railway that started in Camden in front of the Boynton building and went over to Rockland, and there was a spur over to Warren. As late as 1918 or 1919, there were a number of rapid-transit streetcars along the coast. Once you got to Bath, there were streetcars all the way down to Boston. It took time, of course. Life was very slow paced, not what it is today.

Charlie Libby

My grandfather was keeper of the Owls Head light. He retired in 1920. In 1910 he'd moved up from Hancock, where my mother was born. In the 1930s, it was a dusty, ledgy dirt road that went to Owls Head from Rockland. I was only there summers, of course, then. When my mother was in her teens she went to Rockland Commercial College instead of high school. She walked from Owls Head to Crescent Beach—that must have taken her an hour, I'd think. The trolley line ended at Crescent Beach, and she'd take the trolley to Rockland to school. Trolleys, if they went twelve or fifteen miles per hour on that kind of route they did well. I don't know if she made that trip every day, or if she stayed in town during the week.

Those trolley lines from Rockland to Owls Head didn't last long—ten or twelve years. They were abandoned in World War I.

It's funny the things that happen. My grandmother was going to go to Rockland one day, but for some reason she didn't. That was the day the trolley tipped over, and there was a woman killed. It was the only accident on that line.

We were traveling through Thomaston toward Rockland on one of those automobile trips up from New York, back when the trolley car line was still running. The track was usually up the middle of the street in town, and out of town it moved over and ran close beside the road. Father was driving alongside the trolley, and all of a sudden the trolley moved right over— maybe the trolleyman didn't see him. Our car was pushed right over into a tree, and the scar was on that tree until they cut it down not too long ago.

On September 3, 1914, a trolley car from the Rockland, South Thomaston and St. George Railway Company, overturned in Maloney's field between Rockland and Crescent Beach. One passenger was killed and three others were injured.
FRANK CLAES COLLECTION.

Dick Cummings

When I was at Bates College, from 1940 to 1942, I used to catch the trolley to go downtown, and occasionally, just for the fun of it, I'd ride out to Mechanics Falls, Lisbon Falls, or Sabattus. I just simply enjoyed it, that was all. It cost a quarter to go out to Lisbon Falls. What else could I have done with that quarter? (Well, I was just getting old enough to appreciate beer—I could have had two and a half beers for that quarter.) But I made friends with some of the operators, and they didn't always charge me. It was something I could do by myself—no one else was interested. I had a bicycle, too, and sometimes I'd ride that and chase the trolleys.

Forest Bunker
1910s AND 1920s

They had trolleys when I was a kid in Bangor. For a nickel you could ride all over. Just for the fun of it we'd go down to Dorothea Dix Park in Hampden—that's where it stopped—and turn right around and go right back again. It would take two nickels to go to the end of the line, and you could get a transfer and go clear down to South Brewer. A couple of us would do it, 'specially in foul weather. All you had to do was get a milk bottle and sell it, and you'd be in business. They were worth a nickel, and a soda bottle was worth three cents. They had a theater in Bangor, the Olympia, and for a nickel you could go to the movies. So if we had a quarter, we were in high finance.

The trolley was the way to go then. But you know, people walked. We always used to walk downtown. Today you never see anyone on the sidewalks.

Frank Winchenbach
ROCKLAND · 1910s

I used to take the trolley to go to church when I was a little feller. The conductor used to take me by the collar and set me down in front of St. Bernard's. Then I'd walk home, or run. We used to run a lot.

Raymond Pendleton
ROCKLAND · 1910s AND 1920s

We lived up on the highlands. They had a separate trolley that ran out there at that time. Us school kids had special tickets. We generally used them just to go to school with. But unless it was winter and awful bad weather, it was

Electric trolley cars ran until 1931 in Rockland. This one was photographed on Park Street sometime between 1918 and 1924.

COURTESY OF THE OWLS HEAD TRANSPORTATION MUSEUM.

Plowing the trolley tracks in Camden, 1912.

FRANK CLAES COLLECTION.

shorter to walk than to ride. It was just a two-mile walk, or a mile and a half.

They had a big baggage-car thing they used to put a snowplow on. I've seen it buried; they couldn't get through. They had to shovel it out by hand.

Rosella Loveitt
SOUTH PORTLAND
1910s AND 1920s

The trolleys ran from South Portland to Portland from 1895 until 1940, when they were replaced by buses. The early trolleys went off the tracks pretty often, on the curves. It happened once when I was aboard. It just slid off the rail, and there was no great damage. We had to get off and walk home, as I recall. There was better service with the trolleys than with the buses, though, for they ran into Portland every fifteen or twenty minutes.

I recall going over the old wooden bridge that was built in 1823. It was replaced in 1916 by the Million-Dollar Bridge. I would ride with my mother and sister into Portland to go shopping. The trolley cars had their own tracks in the middle of the bridge, and cars and horses would go on the sides, as I remember it. The trolleys didn't always go in the middle of the street; in South Portland, they went on the side sometimes.

I always enjoyed the open cars they ran in the summer, particularly if I could get an end seat. I always thought you could see more from an end seat. My twin sister always liked it, too. If she got the end, I'd sit next to her, and if I got it, she'd sit next to me. I don't remember arguing about it. Yes, we tried to be good.

The conductor went along on the outside collecting the fares. He had a board he'd walk on. There were two people working on the car: the conductor, who collected the fares, and the motorman to do the driving.

In the winter, when they were able to go, they used closed cars. Of course after a bad storm, everything was covered with snow, and they had to wait until the tracks'd been plowed. After one storm, when I was about ten, a group of us thought we'd help clear the snow with our little shovels. We only cleared a few yards, but we thought we'd done a remarkable job.

My favorite trolley ride was always out to Old Orchard Beach. It was only fifteen miles. It didn't take too long—maybe forty-five minutes or an hour—but there were plenty of things to do out there. We'd go on roller coaster rides, patronize the stores, and poke around on the beach. I didn't care too much for crowds, so I didn't go as often as some, but the trolley trip to Old Orchard Beach was the best.

Carl Storer
YARMOUTH · 1920s

My brother and I used to put little stones on the trolley tracks, but the trolley just smashed them. Finally, we put one on so big that it took two of us to lug it over and put it on there, and it made the trolley stop. We only did that once. I think Mother must have spoken to us.

Arlene Storer
YARMOUTH · 1910s

The trolleys used to come by our house. I watched them a lot. There's quite a hill right there, and on slippery days, if they couldn't make the hill, they'd back up and go up the other road. It wasn't so steep by the firehouse.

In summer, they had open cars, and I always rode on the end seat. I liked how the wind blew through. We used to go for picnics out to Underwood Springs in Falmouth Foreside, or Casco Castle in Freeport. They had merry-go-rounds everywhere then. All those summer places are kind of gone by now.

I used to take the trolley in to work in Portland, at the E. M. Lang Company, on Custom House Wharf. Don't ask me how much it cost; it was a long time ago.

Ron Cummings
FREEPORT · 1920s

I was eight years old when they discontinued the trolleys. We lived in town, and my father was a motorman on the streetcars. He baby-sat me many, many times from when I was four years old. If my mother had to go somewhere or if she was busy, I'd go out the door and wait for his car to come along. We knew which was his car. I'd ride with him all the way to Brunswick or even from Brunswick to Yarmouth and back. It took an hour each direction, so I'd be baby-sat pretty cheap! And I loved it.

In South Freeport, the line went up Pine Street, and it crossed Pine Street three times before it continued into Freeport. It was almost always late—they were on a tight schedule—and one time maybe my father was going a little faster than he should have been. He didn't realize that a team of horses had crossed ahead of him and left a good shot of sand on the tracks, When he hit the sand, it threw the trolley off the track and broke a pole.

Another time—I wasn't in the car, but I remember it—my father left Yarmouth waiting room, and he evidently was hurrying. There's a sharp curve there, and he came off Main Street going too fast. The car jumped the track and hit a pine tree and that stove the front of the car all up. That was one of the days

Crossing the Oyster River Bridge to Warren.
FRANK CLAES COLLECTION.

I was waiting for him, and he didn't show up and he didn't show up. Finally, they took over a spare car and my father came along—it must have been an hour and a half later. But I had my ride.

I talked last summer with the last survivor of the motormen. He lived in Bath and his name was Barney. He told me about one time when he was on the top of the hill near the Yarmouth/Freeport town line, and the pole come off the wire. He used up all his air trying to stop—they had air brakes—but he couldn't stop. They had an emergency brake with an old chain on it, and when he tried to tighten up on the chain, it broke. I imagine that when he got to the bottom of the hill, that car was really flying. There's two bridges in Yarmouth—the Marsh bridges, they called them—and one of them, crossing a tidal inlet, was crooked. He said when he hit the first bridge he thought positively the car would tip over, but it didn't, and he continued on until it finally stopped. He put the pole back on the wire and went on his way.

An interesting thing was in the fall, when you'd get a light snowfall, and it would cover the tracks. From the streetcar, all you could see was smooth snow ahead of you, but the streetcar would turn right off where it was supposed to.

I have vivid memories of the trolleys, and perhaps the best was one evening coming back from Brunswick. There wasn't a passenger on the car; it was the end of the line. My father had business to do in other parts of the car, and even though I was just eight years old he give me the handle, and I drove the streetcar up a hill while he was working around the car. Wasn't that something for an eight-year-old boy, let me tell you.

I don't remember that we picked up one passenger all the way back. That was the reason for the demise of the streetcars—people were driving automobiles, and people standing waiting for the streetcar would be picked up by someone in an automobile.

Peg Miller
LINCOLNVILLE

My mother always said, "Someday we'll ride on the trolley to Rockland." I remember when they shut it down. I never got to ride on my trolley.

An open-sided summer car, Warren trolley station.

FRANK CLAES COLLECTION.

Bessie Dean and Midnight Express

Lincolnville

I was born here in 1917. My aunt Avis lived in Lincolnville Center with her son, Walter. Aunt Avis was the midwife for my mother when she had the fifth one, January 5, 1925. I was seven. In the middle of the night—it was ten or eleven—Walter came up to the house with the horse and sled, and we three older ones were all dressed and bundled up, and we rode down to their house on the sled to stay overnight.

It was moonlight and the snow was deep—it always was, in those days. It was pretty but kind of eerie, and it was a mystery to us. It was such a strange thing to be doing, being pulled out in the middle of the night and wrapped all in blankets for a sled ride.

I had homemade skis my father made—he was a carpenter and had his own shop. He made doors and windows, and he could make anything. He put the skis in the steamer and turned the ends up, and he made some leather straps across that we could tie. We were poor and didn't have things like snowshoes, though a lot of people did. My uncle always went rabbit hunting, and he had snowshoes.

My father used to go over to Waldoboro in the open Dodge touring car. He carpentered over there, and we had relatives there. The whole family went, and, my goodness, almost invariably, we'd have a thundershower and have to put the curtains up. And then there was that old Hupmobile we had when I was five or six years old. That was before the Dodge. It had the honker on the side of it. And if it didn't go up over a hill, if it kind of bogged down where it was steep, I'd have to get out and walk, and my father would wait for me at the top.

My uncle had a Model T Ford, and he took us to the movies when I was ten, maybe. It was a silent film, *Ben Hur*. I don't think I went to the movies again till I was in eighth grade.

I didn't go much of anywhere except to

Bessie Dean.
PHOTO BY VIRGINIA L. THORNDIKE.

"The snow drifts were unbelievable in those days," recalls Bessie Dean. *"They just made a little path through."*
COURTESY OF THE ISLESBORO HISTORICAL SOCIETY.

105

school. I used to walk there. Dana Proctor used to live up beyond us. He had an old horse, and he'd go to town for everybody—get grain or run errands for them. They called him "Midnight Express" because it took him all day and all night to get to Camden and back. Well, I was walking to school one time, and he was ahead of me. I caught up with him, his horse was so slow, and I thought, "I'll embarrass him if I walk by him," so I followed along behind for a while. But then I thought, "I'm going to be late for school if I don't pass him," so I screwed up my courage and passed him. He probably didn't care. He didn't say anything to me, just "Hello, girl."

Grammie lived next to the school, and she always pampered me. Kindness was her virtue. I would go in to see her after school, and she would give me something to eat before I walked the mile home. She always had this lemon cake, and there was only she and her son there, so she'd say, "Darling, all I've got is this old dried lemon cake." I didn't care, I loved it.

When the road was so muddy you couldn't go with a car, I'd meet Fred Amborn down at the Center and carry the mail up over the hill for him. There

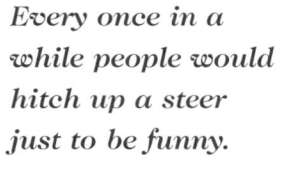

Every once in a while people would hitch up a steer just to be funny.
COURTESY OF BESSIE DEAN.

were five houses up there. I'd carry it for five or six weeks till the mud settled down enough that they could get through. I did that three or four years.

I still walked a mile down to the Center to catch the bus to go to high school. In winter it was cold. Forty degrees below zero once—of course, that was the worst of it. We'd get chilblains. I can remember what we wore in the winter: longjohns—union suits—and you'd fold them around your ankles and pull long cotton stockings over them. Didn't I hate to see that; it degraded my ego so bad. Then we had bloomers, of course, and dresses. We wore leather shoes, and those thin rubber boots with buckles on them—they were really cold.

Virg Hall had an old Page car, and it had what they call monkey seats that came up in the middle or would fold down in the floor. He'd take five or six of us to Camden to high school—we'd pay a couple of dollars a week, as I remember it. There were seven of us in the car the time of the accident, when George Hardy's sister was killed. Somebody came around that corner lickety-cut and crowded us off the road. Virg Hall's daughter was driving, and those cars didn't drive that well in those days. It got off in the gravel and pulled. Yes, I was hurt, too—I got a big cut on my forehead and some on my neck and my hands and arms and everyplace. It made me graduate the General course instead of Commercial at the high school. I just couldn't push the shift key down on the typewriters—they were so hard then—and I couldn't make my forty words per minute.

I can remember wondering if they'd ever pave Lincolnville through the Center. We used to get stuck right where Jesse Warrington lived—there was a big mud hole there. There were a number of others on the way to Camden. (We were awful glad to miss classes, once in a while, though.) They'd use horses to get the automobiles out, if they were stuck bad enough.

I had a girlfriend who lived down on what's now Route 173. I don't know who lives there now—I don't know anyone who lives in town. I could tell you who lived there fifty years ago. My friend's mother always drove a horse and wagon then, and one night she let us take it. I was some surprised. We were fourteen or fifteen, I think. We went up to the Airline Clubhouse to a dance, in North Lincolnville. It was the only time we ever did that—it's a long way. Her mother must have trusted her—and the horse. I was surprised that my mother let me go. We felt pretty big.

Scott Knight had an old truck with roll-up curtains on the side of it, and he delivered groceries once a week. He'd take orders all week, then he'd go around and deliver. He had a big case of eggs and a big kerosene barrel on the side, if people needed fuel for their lamps. He had candy and some other things, too, in case people happened to forget they needed it; they'd see it and buy it.

There used to be a Cushman cart around, too, selling bread and cakes and goodies, but it never came up the country roads or the side roads. People in the village and people who had more money than we had bought stuff from it. My girlfriend who lived on the corner in the Center bought from the Cushman cart. She didn't have a mother, but I did and she baked all our own stuff. We used to swap—my friend liked my homemade biscuits, and I liked her bought bread.

The Transition to Automobiles

Albert Chatfield
ROCKPORT · 1900S

At first, the automobile was a curiosity.

Leda Martin
WARREN · 1910S

We'd get the wagon out and harness the horse—we had a riding horse, so we didn't have to use the workhorses—and away we'd go. I used to ride a lot, too. I walked to the neighborhood school through eighth grade, and then I stayed with my aunt in the village from Sunday night to Friday night when I went to high school. They picked me up with the horse and wagon and brought me home for the weekends.

Our first car was a Model T—it looked good! A car looked good to anyone then. I must have been eleven or twelve. We used to go into Warren or Waldoboro to go shopping, and sometimes I drove the car. I felt pretty big when I was driving. My sisters were too distant from me in age—Gertrude was nine years older, and Maude was six or seven years younger. So I was the only one old enough and young enough to drive it. My mother never learned to drive, just my father and I did.

Frank Winchenbach
ROCKLAND · 1910S

We had a neighbor on Trinity Street who had a pair of black horses. The harness and the vehicle were always shined up good. Then one day, there was a car in the barn with big headlights and a socket to put your whip in. He'd traded the horses and vehicle for a jitney—he was in the jitney business. That was the first car I ever crawled all over, looking at it.

At the Libby Bros. Store in Albion, in 1915, customers arrived both by automobile and by wagon.
FRANK CLAES COLLECTION.

Roy Monroe
MILO · 1920s AND 1930s

There were four different transmissions, the Standard, Universal, Dodge, and Buick. If you had two or more vehicles to drive, wondering which way you went to get into second gear kept you going.

It wasn't unusual at all to see a car with the tires worn down through the layers of fabric. There was a tube inside that. Grandfather had an old stake-body truck that a furniture company had owned, and one day—this is true—I had thirteen blowouts. With four of them, I didn't even get the truck down off the jack. I was getting pretty tired of the whole thing.

Grandfather also had a touring car, and I have a picture of it where you can see down into the third or fourth layer of fabric on the tires. Quite often they'd take a bigger tire and make a boot of it—they'd make some little hooks and rivet them into the side of the tire and hook it under the clincher rims. If you got on a good open road and pulled those things down on both sides, you could kite right along at thirty-five or forty miles an hour even though the tires underneath were worn out.

In those days, the roads were about the way nature intended—you'd go a long ways in sand, and then a little in loam, and a little more in gravel, and then on ledge, and then in something else.

Harmon's Garage was one of three garages in Biddeford in 1915.

FROM THE MAINE HISTORICAL PHOTOGRAPH COLLECTION.

You'd get into a habit, driving a car. Driving in the late afternoon, the bugs would be coming at you, and you'd duck when you'd see insects coming. I still duck. And I go out of my way to avoid a bump; you want to protect your car.

I belonged to a boys' band, and we played at Parkman. We didn't have much money, so we hired what they called a public car to go from Milo to Parkman. It had very wide running boards and open sides. Three of us rode all the way up on the running boards holding on with just one hand. It was all of fourteen miles. I don't think they'd allow that now, and you'd get killed anyhow.

The only airplane I ever rode in was a two-seater. I was in college, and they were there taking passengers up for a ride, and I went to see if I'd like it. I like it—you can see everywhere, and your stomach and your butt are all aligned, and you know where you're going. Not like on trains, where if I start reading, something happens.

We played basketball in Monson. The school would pay for the team and the coaches to be transported over in a vehicle. A trucking company would take a stake-body truck and throw some hay on the floor and throw in some blankets. I can remember standing up the whole trip. It was a torture track if you had motion sickness, and standing was the best thing to do. My eyes were right level with the drifts of snow. They were eight, nine, ten feet high.

THE TRANSITION TO AUTOMOBILES

Isabel Ames
NORTHPORT

In 1914 my father bought his first car. It was a Ford touring car. Later, when he bought a car with an automatic transmission, he had to get used to it, because, he said, he had Ford feet.

Nettie Douglass
DEER ISLE · 1920s

The first time I saw a car was long after I was married. I never drove one. Once I was tryin', and my husband told me, "Now do this, and do that." Then he said, "We're gonna go right into the schoolhouse," and we did! I thought he was gonna help me stop it. I never took the wheel again. They always teased me about going up into the schoolhouse, and I said, "That's what he wanted me to do, and I did it." I thought he was gonna help me stop.

Raymond Pendleton
ROCKLAND · 1920s

I learned how to drive long before I got a car. I was fifteen—you didn't have to have a license then. My father ran a grain store, and I learned to drive on the grain truck. The first car my father had was an old carriage type, with the closed-in sides. He bought it secondhand, a big old Studebaker sedan. There's more metal in one of those than there is in three cars today. The motors didn't stand up, but the rest did.

We had cold winters back then. The harbor froze out so far that the *Ossipee*, the icebreaker, used to come in as far as it could, and my father would hire a pair of farm horses to take all the grain off and bring it ashore. When the boat got to the island, they'd take it off the same way.

One winter it was down below zero for three weeks at a stretch, and sometimes it hit forty below. They had to come in with horses and get the grain—they couldn't get the old trucks started. I wore coveralls then, and I used to line them with newspaper to keep the wind from coming through and biting me.

Gerene Hunt
WYTOPITLOCK · 1910s AND 1920s

I grew up in Wytopitlock, in the southern end of Aroostook County. We lived over a mile from the school. I always walked to school, but there were children that lived out beyond us.

I was a senior in high school before the roads were plowed so cars could use them in winter, but there weren't many people that had cars. There was no electricity—well, the stores and the post office and maybe the barber shop had generators, so they had power. My family used kerosene lamps, and my job was to clean the lamp chimneys.

The hood of a Model T made a good vantage point for one canine.
COURTESY OF THE LINCOLN COUNTY HISTORICAL ASSOCIATION.

Even in summer, there weren't many cars. Not many could afford them. The first time my mother ever rode in an automobile was when I was a little baby. She always used to say the first automobile ride she had, I had, too.

My husband came from Camden, but his sister Phyllis married a man from Aroostook County. They lived in Glenwood, another little town where there wasn't anything, twenty miles from Wytopitlock. There was a little schoolhouse, a small store, and a post office—I don't know if they got mail every day. The railroad didn't go there. Nothing went there.

In the winter, my brother-in-law used to take the scholars to school in a sleigh with two horses. It was a flat-bottomed sleigh, with two sets of runners, front and back, and benches along the side. It had a little wooden house with windows in it, and a little pot-bellied stove. The driver was inside, too. I can't remember how he handled the reins, because he had a windshield. There must have been a place the reins went through.

Braley Gray
OLD TOWN · 1910s AND 1920s

My father had an EMS then later a Chalmers car, and of course they had running boards on them. How we used to tie stuff on those running boards when we moved up to Enfield for the summer!

Enfield, Cold Stream Pond—that's north of Old Town, before you get to Lincoln. There were times the cars would get their front wheels into one set of ruts and the rear wheels into another set of ruts, and you couldn't get out of them for miles.

Charlie Libby

We made the trip from New York to Maine by automobile when it was a real adventure. We had a 1920 Mitchell that was a real beautiful car. It had a bassinet thing suspended from the ceiling, and that's where I was. Even in the thirties it was a two-day trip up from New York. I can't tell you where we stayed. We went through every town. It was quite an ordeal. I can remember one night, we were out there with a match—didn't even have a flashlight—trying to read a sign to see if we were on the right road.

Abbott Pattison
1920s

They had no license requirements to drive a car in Illinois in those days. When I was twelve, I drove a car to downtown Chicago, and just two weeks after my fourteenth birthday, I drove my mother from Chicago to Maine. She didn't drive.

Rena Bunker
TURNER · 1920s

My brother got an old car—I think it was a Ford—and he stripped it all down. All it had was a front seat on the wheels—no body or anything—but we used to go all over the place in it. You didn't have to have a license then. My brother got it in his head to buy old cars and fix them up and sell them again. He died with a lot of money—he was a wheeler-dealer. He became a surveyor and bought and sold a lot of real estate. He used to say, "I don't care about the money; it's the fun of trying to get what you want for something."

The Lamb family and Virgil Hall, Lincolnville Beach, 1914.

FRANK CLAES COLLECTION.

Edna and Went Durkee
ISLESBORO · 1930s

Edna: Remember? I built a fire right in the middle of the road and set out there toasting marshmallows. Ten carloads of people come by, but I didn't have to worry. They'd drive around you if you were settin' in the road, those days.

Went: They'll run you right over now. I've got to watch my chance just to get across the road to my truck nowadays.

Cecil Pierce Reminisces

Southport Island
1930s

I had a friend who wanted me to go to Portland and get a job as a mechanic. When I got there, I went out Forest Avenue to the Hudson Essex place. They was hiring help.

"You a mechanic?" he asked.

"Yes," I said.

In less than two minutes after that, he knew I was not a mechanic, but he hired me anyway. So I did flunky work mostly. We worked on Essex cars—they was a cheaper Hudson. They were delivered on the railroad, with four automobiles in a boxcar—three on the floor and one settin' on its rear end, hoisted up on a ring bolt up in the top of the car. I was in the crew that unloaded those cars and took them home.

We'd take all the jacks and pries and go down to the railyard, which is down on the waterfront in Portland. The cars weren't running, because they had no gasoline in them. We could have put gas in them, but we didn't. We got the four cars out of the boxcar and lined them all up. Then we tied them to each other, and a tow car towed the four of us—strung out—up across Congress Square, right through the middle of town without a bit of a problem. Can you imagine doing that today?

I wanted to get out of Portland, and I'd tried before to get a job at the garage over to Boothbay Harbor, but they never had an opening for me. Then I came home one time, when it was getting well along toward the first of summer. I looked down in the yard and saw it was gettin' full of cars, so I thought maybe he'd want a man. And he did want somebody. I stayed there eighteen years.

But there was no work in the winter. The roads weren't plowed. They couldn't plow them because they had nothin' to plow with, and the cars wouldn't start in the winter anyway. So in the winter I worked on the lobster pound. To get the lobsters to Boston in the winter, the pounds were fished out—we did the fishin'—and we packed the lobsters in barrels that weighed I think over a hundred pounds to a barrel. They had a boat called the *Sonny Jim* that was built especially to carry barrels of lobsters to Wiscasset. From there, they'd go on the train to Boston.

This went on for several years, and my experience with engines at Bill's garage got me the job of runnin' the boat's engine every trip. One year, they thought they'd eliminate the *Sonny Jim* goin' to Wiscasset to the train, and they sent a truck down from Boston to pick up a load and take them right through. The truck backed down the hill—it's quite steep down to the lobster pound—and we loaded her. She never got out of the yard, and she took the bearings out of her tryin'. So she backed down again, and we unloaded the barrels of lobsters, of course. But what were they going to do with that truck?

It was a GMC with a MacKenzie gear in her, so I advised Ed, the foreman, that I used to work on them all the time over in Boothbay Harbor, and I could put new bearings in her. Well, he said they'd have to call to Boston for advice on that. Word came back, yes, they'd let me do it. I never made so much money in my life. I laid on my back in the snow mess there and put new bearings in that truck. Then I come home and told Lucy what a windfall we'd had, because I was goin' to get a dollar an hour. And I think I worked twelve hours to put new bearings in that truck, so I got twelve dollars. It was the greatest job I ever had.

Castor Oil Lubricant

I've been in some awful scrapes. One was over to the garage. Back then—I hardly believe this statistic myself, but I looked it up in a book that I have about it—there was over sixty manufacturers of automobiles—over *sixty* different ones—and they made at least three hundred and fifty different automobiles.

One of our summer residents showed up one day—he was perhaps of foreign descent—and he had an automobile as big as a bus. It was a Sterns-Knight, and that means it was a sleeve-valve engine. He was gettin' friendly and talkin' it up, and he said this was the ultimate car. In those days, you changed the oil and greased the car every thousand miles instead of ten or twelve like we do today. So it fell to my luck to grease it the first time. It had a new type of rear end—by that I mean the back end that drives and sets over the wheels back there. It was a type that's universal today, but it had just come out then, and it creates a lot of heat. The lubricant in that rear end was castor oil. Castor oil is one of the finest lubricants there is, but it has drawbacks too, so it's not used much in that capacity.

So where you gonna get two gallons of castor oil? Down at the drugstore. Now, you know what kind of a rile the drugstore gave me when I went down there after two gallons of castor oil.

The next time that Sterns-Knight come in, the job fell to me again. I didn't always get the grease jobs, but I got that same car and the chance to put in new castor oil. And I thought to myself, I don't think that damn car needs castor oil any more'n any other car. I think it can run on that black grease that all other cars has in 'em. So I drained her out and put the black grease right to her.

But something just told me that I ought to be sure. So I took that car right up the road. I always liked that seventy miles an hour on the speedometer, so I let her have it, almost up to Wiscasset and back. When I stopped down in the yard, the smoke rolled out all around. And that rear end, you could fry an egg on it. I said, I better go get castor oil and change it.

Automobiles Everywhere

Bessie Dean
LINCOLNVILLE · 1930s

Cranston bought a car in 1932. It was dark blue with red-spoked wheels. He bought it new and kept it well. He had it when we first started going out and kept it the first year we were married. Then, you know what he told someone? He said, "I've got to sell my car in order to keep my wife." Oh, he was awful!

Cranston built the garage in 1933—Dean and Eugley's. He was a big gambler—built the garage in 1933 and got married in 1934, in the middle of the Depression. When he had the garage, he bought and sold all kinds of cars. I went to church one day, and when I came out, the car I'd come to church in was gone and they'd left an old wreck for me, with a spike through the gas pedal. I suppose Cranston had traded cars with somebody and sold that car out from under me.

Roy Monroe
MILO · 1920s

When I was in high school I bought a Model T roadster. It was painted dull black, but I changed that to Nile green and painted little signs on it: Watch Your Step, Live Weight, No Springs, and Carry A Nation. 'Course Carry Nation was very important at that time, wrecking bars and what not, so I put an A in it, Carry A Nation, and people were trying to make it do just that, climbing all over it. My father used to say I'd better not go across any side hills, with so much weight on the top of it; it'd tip over. I put some polka dots on it in yellow—it looked fine with the green.

It had a sloping box on the back with covers that you'd tighten down with little thumbscrews. It was supposed to be a crank-to-start, but I used what they

Model Ts

Kits were available to convert a Model T into a snow machine. Lincoln, 1925.

COURTESY OF THE MAINE DEPARTMENT OF TRANSPORTATION.

115

called a hot-shot battery—six or eight dry cells tied together and in a metal case. It had had gas lights, but somebody had made it over to magneto lights. If you wanted to see clearly at night, you'd throw it into neutral and race the engine and the lights would brighten up. You could burn it out, if you weren't careful.

A friend and I took it up to Jackman—that's a long ways off. We'd contemplated going all the way up into Quebec, but decided against it. We kept a log, and documented where we were surrounded by a bunch of cows that had wandered out into the road and didn't want to move.

That car had thirty- by three-inch tires on front and back, to give more traction. They had clincher tires—you'd take a couple of irons and stretch the tire so the beading came out, and then take the tube out and repair it. You could buy a little kit with rubber cement and rubber sheeting, and you'd lay the tube out on a fender—on my car it was flat and was an ideal place to mend your tube.

That car was built the year I was born, 1913. I was fifteen when I got it. I got my first driving license when I was fifteen. They were more liberal about that in those days.

In my Model T, I was the last person to come down a road that at one time was the primary road from Bradford to Brownsville. Every once in a while I'd have to take the ax and cut trees or limbs off and fill washes in. There was one ledge where you'd have had to have dropped down two feet, but I hacked in some dry kindling to level it out.

Automobiles far outnumbered wagons among the vehicles heading to the North Knox County Fair in Union, 1925. Most of these are Model Ts.
COURTESY OF THE UNION HISTORICAL SOCIETY.

Captain Bill Abbott
VERONA · 1920S

My father had a Model T. 'Course you cranked it to start it, and he'd jack up the rear wheels when he started it because the clutch always dragged a little bit. When he got her going, he'd rock her, and rock her off the jack.

That Model T got afire once. He put the fire out with a bucket of water. Then he built a garage out separate from the house.

Charlie Libby
1920s

You were lucky if you got very far without a flat tire or the thing boiling over. And Waldoboro was a killer—you know how steep that hill is, through town? Model Ts had to turn around and back up the hill, because reverse gear had the power.

Rena Bunker
TURNER · 1920S

The first car we had was a Model T. My mother came from down Eastport way—Pembroke. Her father was a minister. She wanted to go see her family—I must have been about ten, and we went down in the Model T. It kept raising the dickens. My father got so mad I thought he'd stave it to pieces. But it worked itself out, and the trip home was fine. I don't remember staying overnight anyplace on the way down. I think we started off early in the morning, and we must have gotten there late in the afternoon.

Captain Bill Abbott
VERONA · 1920S AND 1930S

Spring was terrible—mudholes in the same places every year. There was an awful big one just above our house. Hiram Curtis got a big flat rock and dropped it in there one time, and it went right out of sight. You could get across at night, when it was frozen. Then in the daytime it would thaw out, and people would have to get out and walk around and back and forth and

Mud Season

AUTOMOBILES EVERYWHERE 117

jump up and down to find what they thought was the best place to cross, then back up and give it to her.

Cap'n Roy Meade had a big Dodge with a big set of disk wheels—they had those awful big wheels—and he'd come down through and make the biggest set of ruts. You just couldn't get out of them. Father carried a hatchet to cut his way out if he met someone.

In winter you always carried a set of chains in your car. I did that myself, until not too long ago. I had a 1955 convertible—that's the last car I bought a set of chains for. If it was snowing nasty, you put your chains on. Before you left, the snow would be packed down, and the roads would have five or six inches of hard snow on them. You'd get potholes in the snow. That was the road.

All dressed up and stuck in the mud. Note how the front fender has been nearly torn off.
COURTESY OF EVELYN SHERMAN.

Mud season brought this American Thread Company chain-drive truck to a halt.
COURTESY OF THE MAINE DEPARTMENT OF TRANSPORTATION.

Cecil Pierce
SOUTHPORT ISLAND · 1920s

As time went on, I got a job working at Pinkham's store. By that time I had a driver's license. I'd learned to drive a Ford. We called them flivvers. I was going over to deliver groceries one day. We knew the crossroad was bad. Nowadays, if you was to go through the crossroad and bury the car in a mudhole, you'd be on the road commissioner's throat for having the road in that condition. But I buried that flivver right there in the mud in the spring.

The nearest way for me to get word to Pinkham's was to walk across the woods to Woodbury Love's, the chairman of the Board of Selectmen. I telephoned Charlie to tell him I was stuck in the crossroad. Woodbury couldn't hear very much, but sometimes deaf people can hear what you don't want them to hear. When I got through talking to Charlie, Woodbury turned to me and said, "Well, I hope you're satisfied. You've stove that road all to hell."

Peg Miller
LINCOLNVILLE · 1930s

Mud season lasted six weeks, and you just had to plan on it. We'd bring in grain enough for the hens and the cows and food for us, and then once a week my father would drive a horse down to the corner and pick up the car there and go to Belfast for provisions.

When I started to go to school, my brother was an eighth grader. We used to go to the Heal School, a one-room schoolhouse. Dad picked up nine of us in the car, and in mud season, he'd come down with the horse and a surrey with a fringe. We would all wedge into the surrey in mud season.

The road used to go past our house all the way to Hall's Corner—there used to be a lot of houses in there. In mud season, while Roger Plaisted used to deliver the RD 2 mail, my brother would come down and get the mail for Hall's Corner and deliver it up through, on foot. He'd come back to our house with what he'd picked up from the houses, and then the next day he'd meet Roger with that, and take the new mail from him. It was probably four miles through.

Roy Monroe
MILO · 1920s AND 1930s

People very often would convert their time into money and would work on the roads; they'd quit once they'd paid their taxes. If you had a rock rake going along, towed by a truck or a horse, someone had to be behind with a pitchfork, just to get the rocks out into the ditch—or beyond the ditch, if you could find someone with strength or ambition enough.

People still work to pay their taxes around here; people work in the cemetery for their taxes.

The early roads weren't too much. They'd lay out space for a road four rods wide, but there might just be a couple of cow paths going down the middle, with grass between them and sometimes a rock—it was death on a crankcase. You were apparently supposed to know something when you got into an automobile.

Forest Bunker
FRANKLIN · 1910s AND 1920s

We had a Model A touring car that had those old celluloid curtains you'd put on when it rained—that was deluxe, boy. The roads was what killed you. Hard going. Rough. And mud was a common thing—you'd be going along good, then crash! You'd be in a mudhole. The Canadians had better roads than we did. They had gravel roads where you could see someone coming for two miles because of the dust.

When they tarred the roads, they'd pile eight or ten shovelfuls of sand, and ten feet down they'd make another pile. Then the tar truck came along and squirted out the oil, and young fellows by each pile spread the sand out on top of the hot top. Then a road grader came along, and he'd mix it all up, and then they'd try to flatten it out. Some guys were ingenious: they'd take four or five little birch trees, two or three inches at the butt, and tie them on a piece of timber and run chain from the timber to a drawbar on the truck and haul it down the road. That's how they flattened it out. And

Working on the Roads

How the roads were built: horse and stone boat, men with wheelbarrow and hand tools.
COURTESY OF THE BOOTHBAY REGION HISTORICAL SOCIETY.

AUTOMOBILES EVERYWHERE 119

then you'd go on it with your car and get all covered with tar. That's the way it was done, the only way they could do it, the only way they knew how to do it.

Bessie Dean
LINCOLNVILLE · 1920S

A lot of people worked on the road to work off their taxes. They'd work all summer. Of course it was all done by hand then. People had to be rugged. My father had a big gravel pit, and they'd have a crew shoveling in the pit and another crew on the road, leveling it off as they'd haul it—they had an old dump truck then. My uncle took real good care of his spade. He kept it shiny so he could shovel easy.

Another work crew.
COURTESY OF THE ISLESBORO HISTORICAL SOCIETY.

Captain Bill Abbott
VERONA · 1920S

There were no gravel pits on the island, and they used to get gravel for the roads from the shore. The road they used to get down to the shore was just on the south side of our lot.

Hiram Curtis was the road commissioner. He had a pair of horses and a dump cart, one of those with a pair of wheels forward and a big pair aft. We would ride with him on the high seat of his dump cart. He was a jolly fellow and would sing songs and tell stories to us. The shore where he loaded gravel was referred to as the smelt brook.

He would go down to the smelt brook to get gravel, and of course it was all uphill coming back, so he had what he called topping-off piles. One would be just up from the beach, and another up on the main road. On the last trip up, he'd take all he could off the beach, put on a little more at the first pile, and then top her off as full as he could when he got up to the road.

Distributing calcium chloride to lay the dust on a gravel road.
COURTESY OF THE MAINE DEPARTMENT OF TRANSPORTATION.

Frank Winchenbach
ROCKLAND · 1910S

They used to tar the roads, and I don't know what they used, but we used to chew it. They say you gotta eat a peck of dirt a year anyway, so why not eat it all at once?

Building the Otisfield State-aid Road, 1930.
COURTESY OF THE MAINE DEPARTMENT OF TRANSPORTATION.

Tom Flagg
LINCOLNVILLE · 1930S AND 1940S

I've worked probably on every goddam road in Lincolnville, but not the Number One. That'd been paved in 1934. They were doing that WPA job in Sleepy Hollow, and they was workin' all the time on what's now Route 173. In the winter when it come on a soft spell, it'd get knee deep, and if it froze up overnight, no one could go at all. Frank Hardy would call me up and say, "By God, we better grade it," and he'd get me to drive truck for him.

Most every town had a road grader. The grader had four wheels, and you towed it behind a truck—they used to pull them with horses. It had a tongue you could crank so you could set the front end over and get it in the ditch somewhat. A man rode on the platform. You'd get off and turn the blade by hand—it had two big iron wheels you'd turn one way to lower it and the other to lift it.

We'd take a lantern to work by. From the truck, you couldn't see nothin'—the guy on the grader'd catch on something and he'd be head over

This horse-drawn road grader was converted to winter use by fitting skids beneath the wheels.
COURTESY OF THE MAINE DEPARTMENT OF TRANSPORTATION.

AUTOMOBILES EVERYWHERE

heels before you knew it, so you had to be lookin' in the rearview mirrors all the time. I couldn't see Fred on the grader, so I'd keep checking: "You there, Fred?" "Yeah, I'm here," he'd say.

I plowed snow on route Number One for twenty-five years. I still can't sleep nights if it snows—you get it in your blood or somethin'.

I saw in old town reports where they said So-and-So used his horses toward his taxes. Teams were worth about the same as a man's worth. I always had horses, and I plowed—land plowed—for Collemore, next door. I finally got up to six dollars a day for two horses and a plow and myself. (That was when a man got three dollars.) He thought that was outrageous—just think what he'd say today!

Trucking

Forest Bunker, FRANKLIN

After I had to go to work—you can play only 'bout so long—I worked for a bottling company, bottling soda. Then I quit school. Things weren't good at home. Sometimes you have to make a decision—sometimes you pay for it, sometimes you don't—and I went into trucking. I worked for Boundary Express from 1928 to 1942, and four seasons with the carnival in between.

It was pretty rough when I was driving. There wasn't a good road in the state. They had to make them on a crown so the water would run off, and you was always tipped up sideways. I tried driving buses once, but I give it up. I wouldn't drive a bus again for all the money in Maine. You get a drunk on board, it's a lot to handle.

A 1927 dual-wheeled REO.

COURTESY OF THE COLE LAND TRANSPORTATION MUSEUM.

The favorite truck in Bangor was a REO, named after R. E. Olds—made the Oldsmobile, you know. It was rated for about two ton, but we'd haul six, seven, eight ton. Had to make a living. It had dual wheels on the back, ran 32 X 6 tires. Them things used to blow and scare the life outa you, honest to God. The biggest improvement they've made on transportation is the tires. The front tires didn't have much trouble—the weight wasn't on them—but the rear tires, particularly in summertime, you'd lose them fast. You'd maybe get two or three trips without blowing one.

You were almost always alone. Once in awhile you might have a helper, depending on what you were carrying, but usually you were alone. When a tire blew, you were in trouble. Some guy might come along and give you a hand—we

A weigh station in 1924.

COURTESY OF THE MAINE DEPARTMENT OF TRANSPORTATION.

were always helping each other out. We had hydraulic jacks. The biggest was about five ton, and you'd get them up so high, and *pssshhh*, that was the end of that. A lot of guys carried blocking—you could drive up on it with the good tire, and that would get you up in the air. That was all right if it was an outside tire, but inside, you were in trouble.

We'd run from Bangor to Greenville, primarily, seventy-five miles. We'd carry whatever anyone wanted to ship—groceries and whatever from the distributors in Bangor. We'd go to work at two in the morning and go pick up the ice cream. There were three plants in Bangor that made ice cream in those days. It took three hours to get to Dover, and we'd be delivering from there up. If you got to Greenville at eight in the morning you were doing well. Now you can drive from Bangor to Dover in an hour. The road was there, but there was no bridges, just old wooden bridges some farmer had made out of logs or something. In the spring, the stumps would come up through the road. In those days, if they had a big boulder, they'd throw it in—anything went into the road. Mud season, oh, boy, that was a bugger. Of course they had load limits, and the troopers were always around. In mud season it'd take two trucks to do what normally would be done by one.

Most of the roads had a coat of paving on them, and they made the cement road from Waterville to Bangor in the thirties. That was quite a thing, to build a cement road all the way across there—they were two years doing it. All day long—*kathump, kathump, kathump*—but the cement road was better than what was there before. Like anything, you get used to it, you don't hear it.

Ray Vigue's North Woods

Ray Vigue.
PHOTOGRAPH BY
J. S. ROCKEFELLER, JR.

When I started in the woods, all the work was performed by horses and by hand. Men used an ax and crosscut saw and bucksaw. The chainsaw was the first significant change. The next was the bulldozer; that allowed them to get trucks into the woods. And then in 1973 they stopped the river drive, and that gave me and others a serious challenge.

Haul three cord on a sled with a pair of horses and you're doing well. You have limitations of grade—uphill, the horses can't pull it, and downgrade the sled will run over the horses. With tractors it went from three cord to six or more, and you could go three times as fast at 50 percent of the cost. The darn things don't eat when they're idle, and you don't have to build barns for them or have mountains of hay and grain.

The horse gave way to Lombards. They were big crawler-tractors that had tracks behind and wheels or skids in front. They could pull a heavy load—much heavier than what a team of horses could handle. The first Lombards were built around the turn of the century and were steam-driven; LaCroix used those till 1926. I saw one only once, in 1928. They started making gasoline models in 1909 or 1910. These were faster and cost much less money, although they couldn't pull as heavy a load. Steam-driven Lombards became obsolete. They were slow, cumbersome, and used a lot of cordwood, and you couldn't use them other than for log sleds. The gas models could haul supplies and even build roads—some had dump bodies. They were convertible; you could put wheels on front in summer and skis in winter. The last one was built in 1933, a diesel.

The bulldozer introduced modern woods roads designed for trucks—that's when they started to haul directly from the woods to the mill. Legal gross weight limits increased to around fifty tons in highway service. Off-highway operations on company-owned hauling roads—where only bridge capacity limits the weight—has led to multi-unit truck trains. Some Canadian versions weigh up to four hundred tons.

There's no equipment too fantastic today. You send a man up to the moon, and he gets out into a little jeep and bounces around the surface of the moon, and then you say he'll get back to California at eleven minutes after nine, not ten, not twelve—the technology is there, if you can imagine what you want.

Counting Horses

I was always interested in the woods but I got into timber work accidentally. In 1927, when I was in high school, there was a meeting, and the speaker was Mr. Lanigan, the timberlands manager for the Hollingsworth & Whitney Company. He was talking about the large number of horses they had.

"How many horses do you actually have?" I asked him.

"Oh, a lot of horses. Three hundred, maybe four."

"Wouldn't you like to *know* how many?" I asked him. "If I were a manager of an operation like that I'd want to know how many horses I had."

So they furnished me with a horse for the summer and a long list of camps operated by the company and its contractors, and I rode all over the countryside finding horses. I was paid a dollar a day and found, if you could find it. They paid me for every calendar day, seven dollars a week, and I got a good bonus. I got ninety dollars plus a bonus of fifty dollars at the end of that summer. I was fifteen years old. I loved it in the woods. I love the forest—I always did.

My horse's name was Rosy. She was a six-year-old mare, intelligent, docile, and excellent company. She was a workhorse, but too small to be a real workhorse and too big to be a riding pony. I had no problem with her except once when she was scared by a bear and threw me off. Some days I traveled as much as fifty miles, going from one camp to another. She wore out two sets of shoes; the blacksmith had to replace her shoes twice.

Horses returning after a day's work in the woods.
COURTESY OF RAY VIGUE.

I'll never forget the slushy, sucking sound of Rosy's hooves on a muddy tote road after a heavy rain, or the smell of frying bacon at a camp kitchen at five in the morning, or the absolute quiet at eating tables—other than knives and forks in contact with tin plates. And I remember the smell of horses, manure, and fresh hay at the horsebarn during the evening while teamsters were feeding, cleaning, and rubbing down their horses.

At the end of the summer, I went back to Mr. Lanigan and told him he didn't have quite four hundred horses. "As a matter of fact, you don't even have three hundred. You have two hundred thirty-eight, exactly." He thought he had more than that. "Of course," I told him, "if you're counting horses' asses, you've got quite a few of those."

I had an uncle who worked for LaCroix's foreman, Morissette. In 1928, during my Christmas vacation, Mr. Edouard LaCroix brought Morissette and my uncle to pick up several Lombards. He needed them very soon because he had a lot of wood to move, and he was shy of Lombards. They'd been waiting for sufficient snow on the ground to get permission from the state highway department, because the Lombards had big ice cleats that would destroy the pavement. It was snowing very hard that day. There was probably eighteen inches of snow on the ground when Mr. LaCroix decided to come down and pick them up.

One of the drivers had taken sick with acute appendicitis, and Mr.

Lombards

LaCroix needed a driver to take the machines up to St. George and into Churchill. It was a roundabout way in those days; you had to go to St. George and Lake Frontier and then another fifty miles or so into Churchill.

Matthew Morissette—they called him Matt—and my uncle came to my house and wanted to know if I'd like to work for Mr. LaCroix for the next three or four days driving Lombards up to St. George and come back by railroad by way of Megantic or Sherbrook. I'd never been very far, and it looked like a good thing for me to do, and I said I'd do it. But my mother made me promise I'd be back for Christmas. I had about two weeks to go, which was fine.

So we got the Lombards into a convoy fashion. Mr. LaCroix was in a big car up front. We made it as far as The Forks the first day, and we stayed at the Marshall Hotel. The snow had accumulated to the extent that his car wouldn't go any longer even with chains on. Lombards were very, very narrow-track, and the big car wouldn't track with them. So we left it there.

Travel north of Bingham was very light during winter seasons, and there were few motorcars using highways in that section of Maine until around the early part of the 1930s. We saw absolutely no traffic north of Caratunk other than one contractor plow around what is now Wyman Lake. The highway was very

A steam-powered Lombard log hauler, 1924. Under favorable conditions one of these could pull 24 log sleds at once.
FRANK CLAES COLLECTION.

narrow, and grades steep in both directions and blind curves predominated. Snowfall and winds made driving the slow Lombards hazardous.

We went on to St. George the next day. We stopped at Jackman and ate, and although the international boundary customs station closed at five, Mr. LaCroix had made arrangements so we could cross into Canada after hours. We went on to St. George, and the next morning Mr. LaCroix said to me, "I'm still

A gas-powered dump Lombard with wheels in front instead of skids.

COURTESY OF THE MAINE DEPARTMENT OF TRANSPORTATION.

lacking one driver. If you'll take it up as far as Lake Frontier, I'll go with you, and you could come back with me by rail to St. George, and I'll see you get back home."

It was still snowing very hard, and blowing. We had to leave the road in some places where we had to go around big drifts, through farmers' fields and get back on the road. We finally made it to Lake Frontier. It was 7 o'clock at night, and the snow had stopped. Mr. LaCroix had made up his mind he was going to get to Clayton Lake that night. He said to me, "You've got nothing to lose, the last train has left for St. George. You might as well take it into Clayton and on to Churchill, and I'll see that you get back in time." So off we went as far as Churchill. We got in there very, very late, and he had a supper prepared for us and we went to bed.

It was 245 miles, and the roads were all covered by deep snow.

The following morning, Mr. LaCroix says, "I'm not going back for several days. I've got a lot of work to do up here. Why don't you go with Morissette? Have you ever driven a Lombard with a load?"

I says no, I never drove one in my life until I got into the cab of that one two or three days ago. "Well," he says, "he'll show you how to operate it, and then maybe in a couple of days you can drive your own Lombard, the one you drove up here." So I drove Lombards for eight or ten days.

Delivering them on roads was kids' work; driving in the woods was a different thing. They had a dozen of them where I was working. Horses and smaller tractors would take the sleds out to the main haul road, one at a time, and then link them into trains for the Lombards to pull from there. All the sawlogs went down the Allagash; LaCroix had a huge mill at Keegan, and the sawlogs all went to his mill. The pulp went to Great Northern Paper, so we'd haul the pulp to waters that fed into where the railroad was.

The equipment was used twenty-four hours a day. There was only one man on a Lombard normally—some trips you might have an assistant. We set out at five in the morning and got done at seven at night; then the equipment got lubricated and they made any minor repairs they needed to, and another crew got on and hauled supplies to various camps. Fifty miles was nothing for a sled train—foodstuffs, hay, grain, clothing, and so on. Each camp had a company store, known as wangans. That crew would come back, and we were ready to go to work at five. When things were busy those engines never got cold.

A Lombard wasn't too bad to drive, but the noise was horrible. There were no mufflers, and there were three exhaust pipes sticking up through the hood. It was six cylinders in three banks of two cylinders apiece; each bank had its own pipe. And it was like sitting on a plank—there were no springs whatsoever, no rubber, nothing to absorb the shock. And the only thing between the driver and the engine was the windshield—and if it got hot, you opened that up. You had to plug your ears with cotton when it was working at full throttle.

As far as the driving was concerned, it wasn't too bad. Once you had selected a gear to pull the load, there was very little shifting. A crew spread hay on steep downhill grades—it acted as a brake so the train wouldn't jackknife. You hauled between ten and twenty sleds. They had tremendous lugging power. The only objection that I would have was the mechanical system of steering. That was through a link-chain affair and a drum, and as long as the Lombard was moving, you could steer it pretty well. I was pretty young and pretty small, and when the machine was stopped, especially in deep snow or a rut or something, it was difficult to steer.

The weather was hard. Up there, forty below is nothing uncommon. There'd be weeks and weeks, the temperature never went above zero. You dressed for the occasion—you had heavy fleece underwear, sheepskin pants with the wool inside, and sheepskin jackets. It might be nice and warm in the cabin, but the minute you got out, you felt it. Sometimes you had to wait at jobs while they loaded or made up a train at the point of origin.

On most jobs, an average load was eighty cords, and the speed was two to four miles per hour. Lombards had no speedometers. The top speed was nine, but you couldn't achieve that loaded—you'd throw your load off. A twenty-mile haul was not uncommon, so that was a forty-mile cycle; you could make it in five hours loaded and three on the return trip, so it was an eight-hour turn. (Now we have one man in a huge truck with three trailers moving two hundred cord at forty miles per hour.)

Well, I was having a heck of a time, but I was getting worried about getting home in time for December 25. Mr. LaCroix showed up and wanted me to get ready so he could take me back to St. George and put me on a train. I'd probably have to stay at his home that night with him. "Settle up," he says, "while I get some work done."

I found that after ten days work I owed the company thirty-one cents. I had bought thirty-one cents more than I had earned: clothing, bedding, candy, a shaving kit, all kinds of heavy winter underwear, and so forth. Mr. LaCroix showed up, and Mr. Louida Poulin, the chief clerk, says, "I don't know what to do with this man."

"What's wrong?"

"He owes the company thirty-one cents."

He asks me if I have thirty-one cents in my pocket, but I don't even have a penny. "Well," he says, "we can do something about that. You can go to St. George as planned, but you're not going to stay at my house. You're going to sleep in the jailhouse, and you're going to stay there until someone comes up with the thirty-one cents."

I was worried sick, and I offered to sell my clothes, do anything, and he says, "Unh unh. I've been in a lot of businesses in my day, but I'll be damned if I'm gonna start selling used clothes."

"But I can't take them with me, sir!"

"Well, you can give them away or burn them or leave them here," he says, "but the fact is, you owe me thirty-one cents, and you're not going to be free until you pay me the thirty-one cents."

I was just about in tears—just a young fellow, you know—and finally Mr. LaCroix couldn't hold his laughter any more. He pats me on the back, and he says, "Poulin, you give him ten dollars."

He put me on the Quebec Central, and I went on as far as St. George, where I had to get onto another train to get up to Megantic. There was a line ran out of Portland to Montreal, and at Portland I shifted to the Maine Central and got into Waterville station on December 24 at 11 P.M. It was a long walk home, over two miles, but I got home just in time for Christmas. I had quite an experience, and I'll never forget it.

The Storytellers

Captain Bill Abbott grew up on Verona Island and followed in his father's footsteps as a Penobscot River pilot. He was born in 1922 and now lives in Belfast.

Isabel Ames was born in 1906. Her family home on the shore in Northport has always been her legal residence, although while she was at college and during the thirty-nine years she taught at Hampden Academy, outside Bangor, she was only home during vacations and long weekends.

John "Pete" Ascher was born in 1928 in Minneola, New York. His mother was a Mainer; his family lived in New Harbor for a number of years. He got a job with the Boston & Maine Railroad when he was in high school and has worked in nearly every aspect of railroading ever since. He now lives in Knoxville, Tennessee.

Robert Billings was born on Little Deer Isle in 1905. He grew up there and in Stonington, and spent thirty-five years as the captain at the Indian Harbor Yacht Club in Connecticut. Since retiring, he has lived in Maine and Florida, and most recently in Pennsylvania with his son.

Lawrence Brown was born in 1913 and now lives in Oakland, Maine. He worked for the Maine Central Railroad for forty-three years, and since retirement has been involved with many of the narrow-gauge reconstruction projects around the state.

Forest Bunker was born in Franklin, Maine, in 1910, and worked for a trucking company for fourteen years before getting a job with his first love, the railroad. He was with the Bangor and Aroostook Railroad for thirty-three years. He now lives in Portland.

Harold Bunker was born in 1906, grew up in McKinley (now called Bass Harbor) and Matinicus. His wife, Rena, grew up in Turner and moved to Matinicus as a nurse; there she met Harold, and they stayed on the island for much of their working life. They now live in Owls Head.

Albert Chatfield was born in 1900, and his family summered in Rockport each year. Since retiring from business in the 1950s, he has lived on his Rockport farm and is known internationally as a breeder of Belted Galloway cattle. He liked the early forms of transportation and says, "I've never been in the air; I've never had occasion to."

Ralph Colby born in 1915, he went to sea through World War II and then, like his father, lobstered from Spruce Head Island. He lives next to the lobster co-op on Spruce Head Island and can look out across the harbor and see sixty moored lobsterboats; in 1921 when he and his father moved onto Spruce Head, his father was the only man fishing there.

Dick Cummings was born in 1923. He attended Bates College in Lewiston, and now lives in Manchester, New Hampshire, where he worked for the *Union Leader* for thirty years. He has been active in Kennebunkport's Sheashore Trolley Museum since it started up in the 1940s, but recently he's been just enjoying it.

Ron Cummings was born in 1921. He has always lived in Freeport, where he was in the chicken business until he retired twenty-one years ago. He says he has seen a lot of changes in L. L. Bean's hometown.

Bessie Dean was born in 1917. Her home has always been in Lincolnville. "My husband and I had almost twelve years difference in our ages, but we were as one, and we raised three children, and they all grew up to be decent citizens. Now that they're almost ready to retire themselves, I guess I can say I've done it. That's probably the most significant thing I ever did," she says, "although the most outrageous thing was to learn to fly."

Nettie Douglass was born in 1901 and has always lived in Deer Isle. She raised a daughter, and to this day is interested and up-to-date on the comings and goings of her grandchildren, great-grandchildren, and great-great grandchildren. She is Robert Billings's older sister: "All the Billings family lived to a good old age, bushels of 'em."

Went Durkee was born in Nova Scotia in 1914 and has lived on Islesboro or one of the surrounding islands since he was fifteen months old. His wife, Edna, was born on Cape Rosier in 1921. They've been married more than sixty years.

Tom Flagg was born in 1913 and has lived in Lincolnville since his mother died when he was seven months old. He worked as a blacksmith as well as in the woods and on the roads.

Gertrude Fraser was born in 1916 and summered in Verona as a child. She now makes her home there. She is Bill Abbott's cousin.

Braley Gray was born in 1915 and grew up in Old Town. His family founded the Old Town Canoe Company, for which he worked until his retirement. He lives in Newburgh.

Jim Greenlaw was born in Oceanside, Deer Isle, in 1915. He now lives in the house he was born in, and down the road he has a shop in which he spends a lot of time working with wood.

Francis Haley, known as Fran, was born in 1910. He grew up in Franklin County and moved to Portland and, later, Falmouth. He worked for a grocery distributor until his retirement.

Arthur "Cap" Hall was born in 1908 in Vermont and moved to Greenville, Maine, when he was two. He taught school in Massachusetts and now lives in the Bahamas and Washington state: "I'm working on making ninety. I don't know if I'll make it, but I can remember times during World War II when I didn't expect to see tomorrow, and here I am. Life's a strange thing. Most things that happen just seem to happen—there's no big plan or anything. Some people are very lucky, and I certainly have been."

Doris Hall was born in Massachusetts in 1906 and has lived in Belfast since she was four years old. She taught school for thirty years. Her recurring question is "Why didn't you ask me?" She knows more about Belfast than almost anyone.

Phil Hatch was born in 1916. He summered with his family in Rangeley from 1920 until he graduated from high school. He now lives in Connecticut.

Gerene Hunt was born in 1911 in Wytopitlock. After her marriage, she moved to the midcoast area, where she has lived ever since.

Charlie Libby, born in Rockland in 1923, lived in New York and environs until he was a teenager, when his family moved back to Rockland in the midst of the Depression: "Nobody had anything, but nobody knew they didn't have anything, because nobody had anything." His wife, Margaret, was born in 1918 and grew up in Sandy Point. They both taught in Connecticut and Maine before retiring to Belfast.

Rosella Loveitt was born in 1907 in South Portland, in the house that has been her home for her entire life. She taught school for forty-three years, the last thirty-two at her own alma mater, South Portland High.

Parker Marean was born in Massachusetts in 1912 and summered in Wiscasset as a boy. He lived in the Auburn-Lewiston area while he was working but retired back to Wiscasset. Three of his four children made their homes in Wiscasset, too.

Leda Martin was born in Warren in 1898. She was living in the Camden Health Center when I spoke to her.

Peg Miller was born in North Lincolnville in 1924. She has always lived in the same area of town, although she moved down onto the main road when she married.

Roy Monroe was born in 1913. He has lived in the same dooryard in Milo his whole life. He says he used to think he taught young people—he was a high-school teacher—but he is a little bit ambivalent about it now.

Bill Orr was born in 1923. He took over his father's car dealership in Portland, and after retiring went to work full-time selling boats. He lives in Cumberland.

Raymond Oxton was born in 1913 and lives on Route One in Lincolnville. He has always lived in the same house; he farmed and worked in the woods: "You gotta live one lifetime to learn how to live, and then it's too late."

Abbott Pattison was born in 1916. His family lived in Chicago and summered in Maine, buying property on the shore of Penobscot Bay in 1925. He is a sculptor and painter. During the last few years he has lived on the old family property, although he also spends time abroad.

Raymond Pendleton was born in Lewiston in 1910. He lived in the Rockland area for most of his life. He was in a long-term care facility when I interviewed him. I thanked him for his time, and he replied, "That's all I've got—time."

Cecil Pierce was born on Southport Island in 1907 and spent most of his life there.

He worked as a mechanic, a machinist, and a builder of boats, furniture, and high-end fly rods. His improvement in lobster-trap design was adopted industrywide. He was very interested in local history. He was eighty-seven when he told stories at a videotaped town gathering, and the remarks quoted here are from that tape.

Helen Reynolds was born in Livermore in 1925. When she was ten she moved to Brooks, where she has lived ever since.

Captain Don Rogers was born in 1918 and has been on the water since he graduated from high school. His house overlooking Penobscot Bay has been in his family for two hundred years. He and his wife, Peg, have been married more than fifty years.

Leland Sherman born in 1918 in Northport, lived on Seven Hundred Acre Island, in Northport, and in Belfast when he was growing up. He lives in Lincolnville now.

Richard Sexton was born in 1908. As a young man, he lived in Philadelphia and summered in Camden as often as he could. After several years in banking and in the navy, he became involved in charity work, an interest that continued when he and his wife retired to Camden. He now lives in South Thomaston.

Jimmy Skinner was born in 1919. He has lived in the Rockland area most of his life; his home is now in Rockport.

Arlene Storer was born in 1895 and has spent all her life on the same street in Yarmouth, where she raised two sons. Arlene says she can't remember how many years she worked for the sardine cannery. She is still secretary for the American Legion Auxiliary.

Carl Storer was born in Yarmouth in 1925. A retired surveyor, he moved in with his mother, Arlene, when she was ninety-nine.

Ray Vigue was born in 1912 in Winslow. He has worked in and around the timber industry most of his life and has always been interested in the development and history of heavy equipment. He retired three or four times and went right back to work, but he says this time he's retarded, not retired. He was married for fifty-six years; his wife passed on, and he misses her terribly. He lives in Waterville.

Willard Wilson was born in Cumberland Center in 1929. He went to work for the Maine Central Railroad two days after graduating from high school and stayed with them for forty-one years. Still a railroad enthusiast, he now lives in Falmouth.

Frank Winchenbach was born in 1906. He lives in Rockland and has been in that area most of his life.

Eliot Winslow was born in Boston in 1909; he came to Maine every summer—for all his vacations and whenever else he could—until he moved to Southport full-time in the 1930s. He went into tugboats and still works with his sons in that business.